99 REASONS TO STAY HAPPY

AF566268

MOHD ASAD NAQVI

Copyright © Mohd Asad Naqvi
All Rights Reserved.

This book has been published with all efforts taken to make the material error-free after the consent of the author. However, the author and the publisher do not assume and hereby disclaim any liability to any party for any loss, damage, or disruption caused by errors or omissions, whether such errors or omissions result from negligence, accident, or any other cause.

While every effort has been made to avoid any mistake or omission, this publication is being sold on the condition and understanding that neither the author nor the publishers or printers would be liable in any manner to any person by reason of any mistake or omission in this publication or for any action taken or omitted to be taken or advice rendered or accepted on the basis of this work. For any defect in printing or binding the publishers will be liable only to replace the defective copy by another copy of this work then available.

99 REASONS

TO STAY HAPPY

To whoever reading this,

Contents

Hope this book helps.

Acknowledgements

Hi everybody, this is me Mohd Asad Naqvi, before long be a 20-year-old person. This is my very first book; it's been close to 10 months since I began composing this excursion. It's been a truly extreme one, as ordinarily I understood that I can't do this, I can't finish this book. I need to thank my friend Zahrah Khalid, who brought that little flash from inside me that a little I knew was there. I couldn't ever have finished this without everybody around. My companions, family, I need to thank all of you, for making me complete this excursion.

Foreword

Nothing worth having accompanies a 100 percent assurance of accomplishment, nor would it be a good idea for it. Being willing to face challenges is what's really going on with life.

Living in your usual range of familiarity recoils your reality and gives you limited focus. go out on a limb and perhaps, quite possibly, you'll find the existence you needed 100% of the time.

CHAPTER I

Today's the day you are born

Today's the day you are born. You just opened your eyes scouring them with your little estimated hands, investigating the radiance in the room. Alright, so what's the main thing you do after you're conceived? Cry clearly! So indeed, crying asking yourself what is this spot? Where could you be? Who's this lady in this unusual long free garment (the Hospital garments), for what reason is this man with a major mustache and corpulent stomach grinning at me despite the fact that I'm crying. God, I need equity!!! Hey hello, shhh unwind! You're recently conceived, don't take pressure now since you going to have a great deal of it soon.

Woah! You got your first motivation to be content!

Why stressed when you don't have any idea what's coming. Unquestionably you ought to be miserable on the off chance that you know this "excruciating episode" will occur in your life. Yet, you are no visionary who can anticipate what's to come. So let it be similarly for all intents and purposes, and don't worry on things you don't have the foggiest idea. Obviously, there are this feels familiar, however just know them after they have effectively occurred. Recall rule number one, you don't have the foggiest idea about the future and you can't transform it by the same token. so quit being miserable thinking on the future, rather have a go at fixing your current life, we will discuss this in approaching sections.

• • •

In this book, you'll realize that there are such countless reasons in somebody's life expectancy, Instead, we are trapped in the reasons of being miserable that we never give a look on the positive sides, hopeful reasons. I trust this book might assist you with expanding your motivations to remain blissful.

"Whenever we are conceived, we are making purposes behind others to remain blissful"

How about we expound on this expression.

Along these lines, we as a whole know what's generally significant for our folks, us. Probably the greatest second in their lives is the point at which they are conceived. The planning your mom was accomplishing throughout the previous 9 months is at long last coming at this point. That one second when you open your eyes while scouring them with your hands is the snapshot of affection for your folks. Your first cry is whenever they first blessed, despite the fact that they realize you are crying.

The first time your dad took you in quite a while arms, is the second where he would have felt, that he's the best dad on the planet since "you" came into his life.

That is the explanation you really want to remain blissful, your folks merit this. The principal grin of yours would have made their eyes into tears, the bittersweet tears bliss, the tears of their fantasies. I realize I might sound Apathetic, however you know this family thing. It's passionate 100% of the time.

It's OK in the event that you want to cry on this or there will be consequences on the off chance that you don't, I'm feeling off-kilter now.

• • •

Along these lines, you got one more motivation to remain blissful.

"At the point when we are conceived, we are making explanations behind others to remain cheerful ", recall this state at whatever point you feel helpful, as we as a whole vibe it regularly.

Indeed, when we are conceived we are not equipped for busy, yet something isn't pointless like that. Some way or another or here and there we are doing a great deal, we can't see it.

Being the justification for others grin is the primary thing we did in this world.

The extras your folks purchased with the adoration, is currently sitting tight for you. You show up in the house; you didn't see that you just headed out to somewhere else, as you were resting through the excursion.

The change you acquire your folks lived, is somewhat charming. Your dad finishes his office work with more delight and at a high speed, to make sure he can see you rapidly.

Consistently returning home with another toy, playing with you, sitting close by to see the breaths you take while resting. Your mom dealing with your skin, taking care of, getting you showered, this is the manner by which delightfully you have completely changed them.

They begin seeing dreams for you that they won't ever achieve. That is the way nature plays, they never had some awareness of you back 9 months prior, yet presently you are the most valuable piece of their lives.

• • •

Theirs this excellent statement by Rajneesh (Osho), an Indian public speaker, "The second a youngster is conceived, the mother is additionally conceived. She never existed. The lady existed, however the mother, never. A mother is a new thing". This is so obviously composed, the one who was only a lady before you existed is currently a mother. You gave her the explanation; you gave her this excellent title of "Mother ". The sentiments that she created in these 9 months, the love that developed with you over the long haul made her a mother. She presently holds perhaps the greatest obligation of her life, and she is doing this with the Joy you gave her.

Best of all, you don't have the foggiest idea about this. You are little to such an extent that you don't know to think so. Isn't this the lovely part!?

Turning into somebody's beginning and end and not realizing a Lil piece of it.

Days passed, and you are presently ready to put your initial step on the ground, holding the finger of the mother in one hand and the dad's on the other.

Each progression matches up with the breath of your folks, Blessing every one of your means, consistently there to prevent you from falling.

In this long-distance race of life, there are two defining moments, one when you venture out and the other when you take your last. Falling on the grounds is presently a propensity for yours, however, rising again is the boldness you got to create during the period. All things considered, life is tied in with falling and rising, over and over.

• • •

Indeed, one more motivation to carry a grin to your face, to carry fulfillment to your heart. To cause yourself to associate with this world with each progression on the ground. Keep in mind, with each accomplishment, the youngster makes joy for himself, yet for everything about relatives.

Since it has become so obvious how to walk, you are never going to stop! Wandering from here to there, you have yourself a couple of wings, your mom is presently going to have a full watch on you like a moment prior you were in your room and presently a moment later, you are in the kitchen.

You are catching on so quickly, well incredible occupation youngster! Here is a free tip for the guardians, keep the shiny things far away from you, since they going to break soon!

Presently the opportunity arrives when you express your first word.

Maa, Abba anything it be.

The delight expands, the satisfaction increments. It very well could be a word or simply a large portion of a word, however you said your first word and that is again the lovely snapshots of your parent's lives. They made a decent attempt over the most recent couple of days, to make you talk. In any case, goodness, you little minimal person! You never express a word, you are so inconsiderate! Aa alright no jokes!

Your mother just called your dad, hello need to hear the uplifting news?

• • •

-Gracious would we say we are expecting another??

-Aah no, yet! Be that as it may? Our child just said the very first word!!!

-Gracious truly?

-Can't help thinking about what's going on here?

-Clearly, it's me the dad, loll!

-No, it was mother. Loves me more, hahaha.

-Gracious, that is on the grounds that you are dependably around him/her.

-That was impolite, incidentally.

-Uh oh! Apologies, I'll be returning home early today, it's time to party! Yahoo.

Along these lines, the delight recently expanded, and you began talking that implies you can communicate your inclination?

Gracious indeed, you are realizing one or the other's extraordinary.

So one more motivation to stay happy? Here it is.

You just called out your parent's name, and they are moving at this point! They are flying, your dad is racing to return home and your mother is recording it some place or recording you to make it a memory.

Consistently fresh starts, as time passes you achieving the levels of this life, and you ought to be pleased with yourself.

• • •

In any case, you are little and that you never known about "glad". We never considered liking ourselves, we never liked our doings, we never seen these little

Accomplishments, we never considered giving our back a pat on your back saying, "Great work youngster, you did well back there ". We never did this. At any point wondered why? Why we don't appreciate these "easily overlooked details", you know what; these easily overlooked details matter a ton.

In any case, better believe it, we got reasons. Justification for getting away from the real world, I realize life is extreme there, however seeing these little things will certainly cheer in your life. Let this initial step, this first word from your mouth be the justification for joy all over. Indeed, you should think, where to track down them? The "Seemingly insignificant details ". They are all over the place, they are in your environmental factors, inbreathe that you are taking, in the twittering of the birds in the patio of your home, in the breeze getting through your hair, in the subterranean insects walking towards that opening toward the edge of your home. They are all over, you simply need to take a full breath and feel them. A tip from this part - to begin seeing little things, they will unquestionably carry a grin to your face. We will talk about this in the forthcoming parts.

CHAPTER II

Till the thirteen

Presently, it's been a long time since the day you were conceived. You are developing quick, a couple of months back you began strolling and see, you can rival Usain bolt now.

You feel things, you've fostered your quickly learning memory, finishing the degrees of existence with 5 stars execution up until this point, you've figured out how to develop this much. Presently, you eat without anyone else, you truly do stroll without help from anyone else you run! You have fostered the sensations of adoration, the sensations of outrage, the sensation of being miserable, the delight. Your mom can leave you for some time all alone, the work diminished, however love expanded. Starting your day with fervor, which will in general increment with the death of the day, playing with your toys the entire day, and afterward laying down with no. stress. There is this extremely famous Indian maxim, "Ghodhe bechke sona" importance of this is the point at which the individual doesn't stress over his future or one (he/she) trifles with everything. "Go into a sleep" That is what's going on with youth, not agonizing over the future, about existence, simply living at the time. Indeed, this is a purpose for your grin, this is something that brings a feeling of inward harmony. Overlooking this world for once, and flowing on each "seemingly insignificant detail". That one second can affect our lives so a lot, that we never considered it. A snapshot of excellence, a snapshot of harmony.

• • •

• • •

• • •

• • •

Your first day at school

School, your most delightful snapshot of life, that you preferred not to go to in any case, finished never leaving. Those days were the greatest days of your life, that is consistently there in your souls. The companions we make, the recollections we share are beyond value. What number of you recall your first day at school? For the most part everybody! Firsts are generally best since they are the beginnings. The "first day", the fervor of wearing that new well pressed uniform, the smell of the new books and journals, the calculation box you purchased a day or two ago looks wonderfully created, and have adequate room to place your embellishments in it, the water bottle you need nobody to contact, the dark cleaned shoes, the sack load with a sticker of your most loved hero/ animation on it. It was so wonderful and important. You can pay attention to the transport driver making horn behind the scenes, your mother causing you to have your morning meal in a rush, surging towards the transport and getting on your seat, the wave from your mom to wish you karma for your first day. Each understudy wearing a perfect uniform, you don't anybody, everybody's new. The transport at long last arrived at the school. You ventured your first leg on the ground, the breeze is consistent and cold. The volunteer or the gatekeeper assumed the liability of exploring you to your classes. I recall this adorable second from my life, thus, there was a contest in my school, many schools took part, and there was this lesser dance rivalry I don't have any idea what was the title of this opposition, makes no difference either way. Thus, I was one of the volunteers and I was given the assignment of making the children arrive at their regarded classes. I did partake in the assignment, I felt like I was given a major liability and it was exceptionally adorable, need to

realize why was this charming? It was holding the hands of the children, they were overseen in a solitary line, I was holding the hand of the front youngster, and everybody was following him, it was so adorable. You know what, I felt like I'm their lord, very much like that enlivened series, ' ninja turtles ', where the expert was holding the hands of the turtles.

They moved, shocking coincidentally!

Thus, back to the classes, you entered the class, the dividers excellent painted with kid's shows, a major chalkboard on the divider, there's another board, where graphs of letter sets, names of natural products are appended. Understudies raced to pick their seats, as a youngster the best ones are generally the main column, as they are near the instructor and they notice you constantly. Ok yes! The mystery part, understudy sitting at the main seat generally get chocolates that are dispersed by the birthday kid to the educator, and who denies chocolates!!!

Everybody is caught up with choosing where to sit, while you are pondering who will sit with you. After a second, this kid or a young lady, puts his/her pack on the seat. You are interested to be aware of your accomplice, you never made companions in your day to day existence, however presently it is the ideal time.

You never suspected, the individual sitting close to you will turn out to be so much critical to you, the dearest companion you at any point had. "Ringer rings", your educator enters the class. Great morning mam, this is the slowest and reverb sentence you will be hearing for the following not many years. You won't ever know when these environmental factors turned into a piece of your life when the trees of your playing ground became

companions with you, you share an association now with your colleagues as a whole. The bond you're creating with your closest companion is the explanation you never need to miss a day at school these days. You got motivations to welcome a grin all over each day, that pleasure in singing great morning mam, the unwinding in the wake of seeing that your seat isn't held, the fulfillment when just you know the response to the inquiry in entire class, answering "present mam", with full happiness. The reasons expanded, they increment with all your sections of time, presently you've more motivations to remain blissful. The joy when the educator commends you, the fulfillment of offering your contemplations to your dearest companion, sharing your everyday schedules, sharing your calculation box, this multitude of reasons are filling your heart with joy! Welcoming the grin all over, the harmony in the brain, the fulfillment in your souls, the positive considerations from your educators get you so perked up! The delight of discovering some new information consistently, the fulfillment of recording it in your new spotless note pads with the honed pencil, the adventure of running in external passages, the transport rides, the breezes from those windows, the lethargic rides toward the beginning of the day were so interesting, transport in the first part of the day used to hush up, no quiet, as each understudy used to rest through the entire excursion, the sluggishness in the way back at home, the joy of telling about your day to your folks. Everything for you was new, regular fresh starts, days loaded up with delight, sharing lunch box with companions, those charming battles, the disciplines subsequent to defying any norm, those disciplines of remaining against the divider with your hands straight, each seemingly insignificant detail made the uncountable purposes behind you to remain blissful, for you to remain happy, for you to remain amped up for this excursion.

At any point wanted for a time machine? So you can turn back the clock, to the primary day at school of your life, feels like it simply happened a day prior, time that you've spent in the school was the most magnificent snapshots of your life. Consistently was worth the effort, life is brimming with difficulties, yet we are prepared to deal with each issue cheerfully on our countenances. Guarantee? Welcoming grin on our countenances, similar to we used to move in school as a youngster.

• • •

• • •

• • •

• • •

Your first test of life

The first-ever test of your life. The very first trial of your life. How was it? We as a whole progressed admirably. The environment, the strain, the tension that used to be made naturally before the test. Feeling strained a day prior to the test, felt like a day prior to any judgment found in the motion pictures. The second you enter the class, you begin hearing the sound 'tick-tock', the clock of dread uttering the sound of dread. Those most recent couple of minutes prior, the test was the main time frame, as your brain use to work at 4x speed, printing each sentence that goes over your eyes in that period. Hanging tight for your companions in the passageway, and inquiring as to whether they gave considered or not, and afterward they answering with their resonant falsehood, is there a test today!?

The second where our mouth closes and we communicate everything with our eyes is the point at which the invigilator request that the understudies keep their sacks out of the class. The second when our eyes covers get greater, gazing at our companions, to wish them 'the very best!'. The time has at last shown up, the invigilator is disseminating the paper now. you are as of now strained before seeing the inquiry paper. Imagine a scenario in which the paper is extremely intense. Imagine a scenario where you don't recollect the responses. Imagine a scenario where you can't complete it on schedule. Giving a gander at the paper with one eye opened, you read the inquiries. There are just different sides, on the off chance that you know the responses, you won't ever know where the time went, and second, when you don't have a clue about the responses, god! Just that individual knows how he endure those two or three hours.

In the wake of composing all that you know, presently the opportunity has arrived to ask your companions. You begin moving your head, attempting to get a look at their papers. Making a decent attempt so they can see you, you make a commotion. At last, they saw you. Indeed, you should be great at cheating, else you would be gotten. It takes guts to cheat, alright jokes separated!

Applying your lord procedures to swindle the responses, you are at last finished with your paper. One of the entertaining minutes during the test was to check the response of your companions, who are as yet composing; when you are finished with the paper. That fulfillment is so malicious and interesting as well. Holding up external the class, for your companion to complete the test and asking, how was the paper, to which they answer, come up short hoon Bhai (fall flat, sibling) is the joy that carries a grin to your face. "The way that, " I'm falling flat, however damnation yes not the only one, my companion as well" is the fulfillment that made your unpleasant day an insane one. The strain, the tension, the 'tick-tock' to you, the cheating, seeing individuals requesting supplements when you are still left with your initial one, all made up your day, probably the best snapshot of your life, the second that will continuously bring, a grin all over, the second that will unquestionably make you dismiss your butt. Now and again stamps don't make any difference, what is important are the recollections the chuckle that you made, the minutes you made that day. As these recollections will remain with you in your souls until the end of time. The apprehension about the test used to hit different in those days, returning home after the test, when your mom asks

you "how was the test!? Answering to her " It was magnificent", in spite of the fact that you know the truth behind it. These minutes we probably won't see in those days, yet presently we need to encounter them again in
our lives. Watching understudies talking about whether the response was 200 or 200 and one, while there's you who found the solution '59 point six', these are the minutes you need to live once more, one more motivations to welcome a grin on your countenances.

I need to share this second, when I was in class seventh or eighth I presume. In this way, a companion of mine wanted to keep a book in the washroom, he did in like manner. Yet, the part where he did everything wrong was that there was his name on the book and he didn't delete it or made cut with a pencil property. Everybody was composing their paper and out of nowhere our p.e instructor thumps on the entryway with this book he found in the washroom. Fortunately, he couldn't spell the name as it was not satisfactory, what was composed. Yet, the person whom book had a place with was dead. So indeed, this second made me ignore my butt, then, at that point, it actually does. Assuming that you are as yet in school, make recollections, notice little minutes, on the off chance that not in school then, at that point, recall these minutes at whatever point you feel annoyed or discouraged cheer those minutes, you have your motivations to remain blissful. We don't have to search because of motivations to remain cheerful, they are in our environmental elements, they are in our souls. We simply need to see them.

From the day you gave the test till the outcome day, you are generally as it were of dread. All things considered, it's human instinct. We generally stress over the future,

despite the fact that we shouldn't. As god has composed the best for us all, and agonizing over it won't transform anything, with the exception of expanding our pressure, clearing your grin off of our countenances, and placing us

in wretchedness. All we want to do is to get ready for it, rather than stressing we should buckle down for it, to accomplish our objectives.

• • •

• • •

• • •

• • •

• • •

• • •

The day you made friends

How old would you say you were, the point at which you made a companion? How about we go on from "your first day at school" When somebody sits close to you, You at last got your accomplice, seat accomplice I would agree. In the event that you are not modest, then, at that point, making companions is no biggie for you, yet in the event that you are a bashful, independent sort, gracious god! This is the hardest occupation of all time! Me being a self observer find it somewhat difficult to make companions from the outset. Contemplative people are enduring rocks and I don't joke around about this, you need to make a decent attempt to be companions with us, yet yes we are the best from inside once you get to know, alright enough self-fixation, simply kidding. You need to circumnavigate around them for a really long time, similar to those talks where somebody composes a long passage and different answers 'alright'. Thus, I was a self-observer and you know what I changed four schools, well the first was a grade school, so in fact three. Also, it was extremely difficult for me to make companions as at whatever point I figured out how to make the bond more grounded, I got moved to another school. goodness!

We should discuss my first school, I made a companion there, we use to trade our tiffin boxes, what's different here is that, he was never permitted to eat noodles, so his mom never gave him noodles in the lunch box, on the opposite side, I use to bring noodles frequently. So we use to trade our tiffin boxes, his mother was great at making frankfurters. Fortunately, I'm still cordial with him. In the subsequent school, I have left without any companions once more, and coming back home on the absolute first day, this person was pursuing me, I saw nothing and when I was eating mangoes at home, somebody thumped at the

entryway and it was him. He tracked down my home, what a government operative!

That was the day we became companions, no companions except for dearest companions. He turned into a justification behind my grin, generally their sort of a person. I realize you are understanding this, a debt of gratitude is in order for being a major piece of my life. Kinship is the greatest string in somebody's life, it can bring the change that perhaps nobody would be able. In a month, I made a pack of mine, 'AAO' posse!

Gained heaps of experiences, each memory has its huge story behind it. We are will speak more about this, we should get to my third school, it was an insane ride, from the earliest starting point as far as possible. I got confirmation at the hour of the half-yearly tests. In any case, the great side was that I knew not many of the understudies there. Didn't took long to make a group there, once more! Making recollections, minutes I delighted in. However, the way that I always remember the past ones, unique stories, various recollections, various stages, grins that will remain perpetually with me. The second you enjoyed with your companions is precious, anything that your disposition is they will transform it with their inept jokes. Experience those minutes.

There's this truism by Muhammad Ali, "Kinship is the hardest thing on the planet to clarify. It's not something you learn in school. In any case, on the off chance that you haven't taken in the importance of companionship, you truly haven't gotten the hang of anything".

This is so evident. Fellowship is a feeling that is created in us naturally. Making a companion isn't hard, yet keeping up with the bond is hard. We make a great deal of companions in our lives, however just a few become our dearest companions, the one's we had the option to keep

up with the bond with time, making the bond more grounded with time. Battles happen when there is valid companionships, the battles you will recollect, the embrace after the battles were the medication to your aggravation. Your closest companion generally know what's going in your mind, that is the thing genuine kinship is, life is excessively short, we shouldn't squander these minutes, an opportunity to make recollections. That evening stays, the gatherings, bunch studies, the lengthy drives, birthday bombs, the mystery talks, the late-night arrangements, acting guiltless before one another's folks, sharing, consistently there for one another, offering guidance on affection yet are single themselves, the disciplines together, and uncountable recollections, to fulfill you for eternity. Kinship is a gift from God to carry purposes behind you to remain blissful.

•••

•••

•••

•••

•••

•••

•••

•••

•••

•••

•••

•••

•••

•••

•••

The teacher

We all have a teacher in our lives,or anyone who any individual who gives you the right knowledge regardless of whether we haven't gone to class. An educator can be all over, you can see an instructor in your mom when she never allows you to do anything wrong. You can observe an educator in your dad who guides you about the straight way, the way he has experienced, about this hard life, the ideal decisions. You can find an instructor in your companion as well, who offers you guidance, consistently there to help you. An instructor isn't simply a pretended by a few specific individuals it's a word for truth, a word for the best thing, a word for motivation. As a kid, we never thought about this, all we needed was the ringer to ring so the period moves past and the instructor is no more. Indeed, we don't have development in those days so I surmise that we are not to be accused. With time, we change and we get kind of interest in the examinations. Numerous understudies got a pulverize on their instructors, would you say you are one of them? Ahem! All things considered, there's no off-base, we can get a pound on anybody whether it depends on their looks, their voice, their fondness towards you or their instructing style. You begin looking into the investigations more when you begin preferring them. Continuously lifting your hand to offer them the responses, never missing their classes are the best second we as a whole grew up with, and will recall for eternity.

A decent instructor can assist you with carrying a grin to your face, help in getting you on the correct way of life, giving the right training, making you roused consistently, fostering your psyches, preparing you for the cutthroat tests out there, acquiring positive energy you, a decent educator can bring such a lot of progress in your life that you won't ever consider. Allow me to enlighten you

concerning a few instructors that completely changed me. In my first school, I loved my English instructor due to how she manages the understudies. With such a lot of straightforwardness and a vivacious mind-set, she generally carries inspiration to each understudy. Obviously, she was great at educating and she uses to make us liberated from our troubled psyche, by messing around and some of the time orchestrating secret gatherings in our homeroom. I recollect that, she organized a class party for understudies of our group just, it's been all the more right around a decade since that day, however I actually recall. It was an excellent memory for me. I partook in the day, and I want to in any case return to that time. You will always remember a day all around spent, a day you made a memory, a day you giggled so hard that your eyes were loaded up with tears. I met a great deal of tears, as you realize that I examined in three schools. Yet, aside from that, an educator who changed my life isn't from school. Above all, read this excellent statement, "An instructor sows the seeds of information, sprinkles them with adoration, and calmly supports their development to deliver the upcoming dreams." - Unknown.

Presently, we should discuss my educational cost/instructing classes. I was in the 6th standard when I began going to the training. Well it was is instructing focus, it is a home guide place. Furthermore, best of all, it is before my home, we are neighbor's before I was conceived I presume. In this way, she's an old woman and she is the best instructor I at any point have. Maths was the main subject that I use to concentrate on there as she's a maths educator. In prior days, I never enjoyed going there, clearly who likes to study and furthermore when it's maths. I was the main junior understudy there, and everybody was senior by four or five years. With time,

new understudies came. Understudies of my age, my clump and I began appreciating going there. The exhausting everyday practice of going to the educational cost was currently different to a great daily schedule. We use to read up for quite a long time with no sluggishness by any means. Here and there our instructor used to recount a story, and obviously, who would rather not have some time off, all things considered, it's maths. We, understudies, use to illuminate her about the petition at the specific time, so when she goes to offer her supplications, we can have our discussions unreservedly. Taking water breaks, eating the food brought by an understudy for her, the discussions in soft tone behind the scratch pad, not needing our vast discussions to end, are the excellent minutes that were made. How she (the educator) use to rebuff us by sticking our hands gradually and delicately, perhaps that is the reason we the understudies needed to do the slip-ups.

These were the occasions, the explanation, that carried a grin to my face. It seemed like my spirit getting sanitized when she use to instruct. The manner in which she showed us, I never imagined that maths could be this simple. I was a sub optimal understudy in maths however subsequent to gaining from her I figured out how to get a 94 out of 100 on my sheets. Nearly, the most elevated in my school. Consistently another explanation, to remain cheerful, to remain invigorated, to discover some new information happily of pride. That is the reason we ought to constantly search for these 'easily overlooked details' all over the place. They are all over, the reasons are all over, bliss is in the air we simply need to take a full breath and cheer with our grins. There's a statement, "Better than 1,000 days of pleasure study, is one day with a decent educator".

An educator holds perhaps the greatest obligation of the world, the obligations of getting you towards a decent way, acquiring the delight of information your life, making you grin by his/her helpful discussions, to get the best out of you.

• • •

• • •

• • •

• • •

• • •

• • •

The lunchbox

We should begin this when we were in grade schools. waiting that the period will move past, the chime rang, yes it's noon. All the students opening his/her lunch box, with the energy, the desire to actually look at what's in the box today. The majority of the lunch boxes, contained noodles, sandwiches, paranthas, and so on The room used to get loaded up with the scents of the food sources. Asking your companions, accomplices, what's in their lunch box today? these minutes were so adorable. Never thought sharing these lunch boxes with them will make us share our insider facts with them one day. The bond will turn out to be so solid with simply sharing the lunchbox. These various shades of lunchboxes, the greater part of the understudies use to bring that Tupperware plastic lunchbox and everybody used to be like goodness, he is the Tupper fellow. These were a few understudies who used to brought those enormous lunchboxes, the principal layer for organic products, the second one for some sabzi, the third one for the chapatis, fourth one for the rice! The hurrying or understudies through the hallway, a second after the chime rang, made you so lively. Sitting tight for the break, pondering what's in the present menu in the bottle. Back in my school, our flask's menu used to be a Nathus level menu. Mondays and Fridays for Rajma chawal, Tuesdays were my #1 day as the flask used to save pav bhaji, Pav bhaji is my number one, one of my top picks I would agree. Biryani is generally number one in food sources. Unfortunately no biryani on the menu of our container, yet veg pulao for its sake use to be served. who says veg pulao biryani well Wednesdays would i say i were don't recall that perhaps Chhole kulche there would one say one was more - that used to be awesome on the bottle likewise I have never known about anything like this

before it was at Chaumin ka samosa yes knew about this name? Do it was probably the best thing I have at any point tasted you should taste it once in a daily existence. the battle we need to do, to get that Samosa was an amazing experience. the battle used to welcome a ton of grins on our faces used to disseminate our days with the goal that one person daily will proceed to carry the food to us. feels yesterday ordinary spend at the container is so noteworthy the occasion were so precious container has been a major piece of our lives, the arranging that structures made at the back the battle that started in the classes and finished there, the commitment of cash to get the stuff to eat, the birthday celebrations and loads of tomfoolery. the association you accept with the bottle rib bhaiya. the thought process behind composing this section flask was to cause you to recall your bottle days assuming it did as such I am extremely delighted to cause you to recollect your past times. I recall that there was everybody's proper spot close to the bottle like what we call adda in Hindi. Where your posse or companion accumulate for discussion, where you made recollections, where you made explanations behind a grin. There's a delightful sonnet by Abhilash Pillai,

A place of everyone's dream
Where college always seems green
With all jubilation among the teens
Yes, it's our 'Canteen'
It's every evening's routine
Girls chatting about their things
Each of them dressed like Queen
Enters the only place 'Canteen'
Boy's activeness shows its grin
Silence diminishes, as it never had been
Dominates surroundings of 'Canteen'
Eyes searching for their favourite beings
If succeeds, celebrates the win
Praying to have the everyday same scene
Leave the place of Love and Life 'Canteen'.

• • •

• • •

• • •

The fictional world

Alright so presently we will discuss the most vital snapshot of our adolescence. The 'fictitious world', by fictitious I mean the world that was not genuine. Indeed, I'm discussing kid's shows. "The permanent snapshot of our life".One of the reasons we needed to complete the classes in school was to race into the couch and gorge our #1 animation shows. Inclining toward the couch till early afternoon, actually wearing the school uniform while your mom shouting from the foundation "change your uniform!!! ". Be that as it may, you are lost, lost in the dreamland. A large portion of our number one kid's shows would be tom and jerry, Doraemon, shin chan and there was this startling animation show "Mental fortitude the fearful canine". I use to get frightened of it, cuz no difference either way! It was the most unnerving animation show of that time and the timings of the show use to be late around evening time around 11 PM, so for the most part I use to fall asleep. There being lost was not terrible. Lost in the realm of dreams, admiring the characters and depicting them as they are genuine. Purchasing the product of your #1 animation character. However, the wish that you create in your heart, that one day I will meet that character later realizing that they are not genuine was a mistake. I recollect that I was exceptionally attached to the ben 10. So on one occasion I purchased his watch called 'Omnitrix see I actually realize the name henceforth demonstrated a major fan, haha!

So I got myself this Omnitrix and the most clever part is that I was expecting that it will transform me into the outsiders like ben use to. Following an hour of turning the Omnitrix was at last ready to realize that it was false. Yet

was appreciative for it to make my youth astounding. The activity use to be lovely to the point that everybody

watching it use to become mixed up in it. Trusting that the following episode will know what will happen to ben, who kill the primary miscreant were the rush that I use to snare on and that rush use to give a great deal of joy to my face. Those conversations in the free times of the school, investigating our number one characters to prevail upon the other's #1. The days use to be brimming with pleasure. Trading the activities figures with your companions, suggesting the kid's shows, examining the impending episodes of them, drawing your optimal characters, dreaming on the off chance that you get the Doraemon, all things considered, life would be so natural. Utilizing the devices to finish the tests with the best grades, winning each battle with the awful kid of the class, no issue in venturing out from home to school as you got the bamboo copter, making your crush go gaga for you, being simply the coolest person of the school, making yourself all that you at any point needed, yet a fantasy thought. Was a fantasy, yet you appreciated dreaming it, you partook in the grin it gave, the joy of being into that dreamland.

Getting up from the get-go the ends of the week just so you didn't miss your number one animation was without a doubt the best fervor we at any point had. Weeping for the toy that you just saw in the shopping center and cause your folks to consent to get it for you. The days were so honored. In spite of the fact that they are simply characters made by people himself yet the connection that we create with them is on another level. The makers made these from their persona of them, the Joyce that they miss now from their lives, the person they generally needed in their lives, they made it for us. The majority of us actually love to watch kid's shows, since we are joined to their number one characters or for a few different reasons.

They turned into a piece of life and it seems like they were consistently there. You long for them, they rouse you in

numerous ways. So as an aggregate, the imaginary world plays had a major influence in our lives. Making our adolescence paramount, welcoming grins on our appearances when we were not in the disposition. Transforming your attacks giggles. Fostering your creative mind. Transforming our drilling days into perhaps the greatest day of life. Freeing the dance once again from you at whatever point the introduction played, coincidentally, I suck at moving. So I would it in the care. Learning the importance of connections, kinships from them. These were a portion of the excellent snapshots of your lives, that give you huge loads of motivations to carry a grin to your face.

• • •

• • •

• • •

• • •

• • •

• • •

• • •

• • •

• • •

• • •

• • •

• • •

• • •

• • •

• • •

• • •

Sleepy nights

So at long last you came to your most loved sluggish movement, well not completely lethargic yet some of the time. We as a whole have been to that period where we use to adore dozing, I'm not talking that we as a whole need to rest as it's self-evident. We as a whole need to rest and we love it. However, here from affection to rest I mean, dozing with next to no weight on yourself. The delight of not working somewhat more longer in the wake of switching off your disturbing morning timer, pls let me rest a little morning timer, don't act like a servant who switches off the fan each time I'm in a wonderful drowsy dream. My resting position use to be extremely bizarre those days, as genuinely dozing straight and winding up in a horsey position, spots of spit from your mouth on the pad, gracious gross! Ew, yet yes that was an indication of good rest and I'm almost certain you would've encountered this thus does each human most likely. So if in these intriguing, pushed days you got an opportunity to make your pad grimy with your spit then congrats you are resting soundly. All things considered, it is valid, that nowadays resting soundly has turned into a bonanza in our lives. Focused and discouraged days have made those evenings lost some place. We have made ourselves such an excess of associated with these world issues that we never care to finish the rest. Recall the days, when we never wished to get away from the fantasies? never needed to put alerts so we can get up upset consistently

so what's the distinction now? We are as yet unchanged individual, I intend what has rolled out the improvements in us, that we turned out to be totally various individuals? At any point posed this inquiry to yourself?

The response lies in you.

We have begun treating each seemingly insignificant detail so in a serious way, that we get such a lot of associated with those. Winding up Ignoring each energy in our lives.

allow me to take a model, there is this man who works in a 9-5 work, gets back home consistently with a focused on face. His family begins asking him inquiries, how was your day? youngsters' asking, did you presented to me what I requested? With a mad outburst, you said them to be calm or to don't inquire. He got it done, he lost the little joy his kids were hanging tight for, or you can say he lost the joy he would have encountered on his kids' appearances. The things that you were causing you to feel aggravated, made you disregarded the very thing that would've been a fix to this bothering. Allow us to say these Irritational sentiments or pushed minutes. So this implies these focused on sentiments cause you to disregard the better things as well as make more issues and subsequently deducting a great deal of the numerous seemingly insignificant details from your life. These focused on sentiments are affecting your life in the long haul, issues brought about by this can most recent 10 years after the fact in somebody's heart who was wounded by certain lines constrained by pushed sentiments.

That is the way most connections are screwed up these days. Hearts are broken by these focused on sentiments which makes a great deal of disarray between one another. We never realize the amount it can offend someone except if we experience it ourselves. We understood these things later, however at that point it's past the point of no return. So your focused on feeling has made a significant issue obliterating your relationship, which was the justification for your numerous easily overlooked details, huge loads of little reasons, to make your tears wipe away. To carry a grin to your face. Reasons you were carrying on with your life on. Presently huge loads of reason has been deducted from your life since you were so much associated with your focused on sentiments. Which has now made another discouraged inclination. We will discuss connections in the impending section. On the whole, let us consider what need our rest has meant for us perilously. Focused on sentiments can be of many sorts, the sensation of forthcoming office work, not calculable compensation, not having the option to gift your significant other that accessory which costs double how much your compensation, future plannings, and so on A great deal of senseless pushed sentiments have made your eyes get up till late.

Have caused you disorder of absence of resting, have caused your downturn, awful wellbeing and an augmentation in the displeasure which ruins the entire thing. Seemingly insignificant details can have a major effect on your life on the two sides. It is possible that it is positive or negative. Rest assumes a significant part in deducting these focused on sentiments, a decent rest can decrease your downturn, it can make you fit, it can eradicate the dim heads under your eyes and can increment greater inspiration in you. That is the justification for why we use to go into that endless rest in our adolescence since we didn't use to treat these focused on sentiments so in a serious way. Therefore we have been feeling the loss of our drowsy evenings, so toward the finish of this subject, I need to say that, somethings are made to be disregarded, we shouldn't approach those things in a serious way which can turn into motivation to deduct motivation to grin.

• • •

• • •

• • •

• • •

• • •

• • •

• • •

• • •

• • •

• • •

• • •

The Peddles

Have you at any point rode a bicycle? A large portion of you would've, so in a bicycle with all your means, the peddle goes up and the other down and again it rises and goes down, making you near your fate. It is very much like our life, the sells are the means, the high points and low points of the bicycles look like the successes and disappointments of life. All Your means in life implies a ton. Presently let me recount to you a story, I read on the web.

Quite a long time ago, there was a 12-year-old kid, Ahmad. One evening, when he got back home he was exceptionally eager. He requested that her mom give him something to eat. Her mom addressed my dear child, we don't have anything to eat. Ahmad's dad was an unfortunate man. His dad strives to acquire bread and butter for his loved ones. Whenever he gets work, he carries food to his loved ones. At times he neglects to look for employment and gets back home with void hands, that day turns into a destitute day for them. The synopsis of their monetary condition resembled either track down a job or starve.

At the point when the mother told Ahmad, they don't have anything to eat he turned out to be extremely miserable. He stayed quiet for some time and continued to think. Then he told his mom, don't you even have 5rs. Her mom said, let me check. Then, at that point, following a couple of moments, she accompanied 5rs. Her mom said, Ahmad how will you manage this minimal expenditure? It has no value. Ahmad said mother I have a thought. He took 5rs from her mom. Then he took a can and filled it with water and told his mom, don't stress I will be back in a brief time.

Ahmad went to a shop and purchased ice with 5rs. He added ice in water and remained external the Cinema Hall to sell cold water. It was an exceptionally hot day and everybody needs to drink cold water. He began to sell cold water and his water began to sell rapidly. In 1 Hour, he sold the total pail of water and procured 500rs. Presently, he begun to do it everyday after school.

He proceeded with his diligent effort for a considerable length of time. Helped his dad in procuring bread and butter and on the opposite side he proceeded with his schooling. Then, at that point, he graduated and found an excellent line of work. His month to month pay was 50,000rs. He proceeded with his evening business too. With his battle and difficult work now, he is carrying on with a cheerful existence with his loved ones. Presently, they are moved to a fresh out of the box new house. His folks are exceptionally pleased with their child.

Troubles can turn into the justification for progress. Yet, one should never allow these hardships to beat him down, all things considered, they can turn into the wellspring of assurance. The genuine article is life to steer a positive development.

Propel yourself, no other person will do it for you. Begin your excursion with "5rs" You have. Since it is the main thing workable for everybody. Each excursion which is begun with "5rs" can turn out to find actual success. Thus, begin with anything you have, any place you are and gain an illustration from this Motivational story of an effective individual. To accomplish your objectives you should need to move toward your objective.

CHAPTER III

Let's talk about love

THE CRUSH

Here we are, to our most aniticipated piece of our life. The part you've been holding up from the very beginning right? I had many crushes, a great deal of them yet on the off chance that you are accepting squashes that are far past our limits, the ones we couldn't actually talk before, that main few. I also was a timid humiliating person, okay I actually am. The day I saws her, I actually recollect it. The sluggish motioned look, scent of affection all around, an expansion in the size of the moon, a delicate and eased back tune being played behind the scenes, that is generally very Bollywood, nothing really occurs, all things considered. In any case, indeed, the heart beat my god, that thing is genuine sibling. This piece of our life, is one of generally delicate one and adorable. we make bunches of smashes and we let them go, exactly the way that we let go a great deal of things throughout everyday life.

Adolescent years are one of the most astounding as well as befuddling seasons of one's life. During circumstances such as the present, you really begin seeing the contrary orientation more than just "Cohorts or Schoolmates".

"a brief but intense infatuation for someone, especially someone unattainable."

I read this some place and it's perfectly written.

• • •

• • •

• • •

• • •

Fundamentally, this is whenever you first foster a Crush on somebody. What's more, from individual experience, I'll let you know that it is in a real sense the best experience of all time.

You try not to play Truth and Dare with her. You know why! The most well-known Truth question is "Who is your crush?" It's essentially simple. Allow me to let you know one more abnormal snapshot of my life, I played truth dare with my crush alright I concur, a large portion of my choices are awful. Thus, sadly she asked me "Who's your crush", believe me this is one of the most abnormal second in somebody's life. Your crush asking you who your crush is!? You'll get astounded to my answer, I answered "You". She was stunned like truly, she asked this once more "Me"? Her eyes were practically out of the lateral rectus muscle. I somewhat felt courageous. Alright we should get back on the track; I'm beginning to get off-kilter once more.

You make a decent attempt to get to know her companions just with the goal that you persuade a reason to associate with her more regularly.

You see each and every other person conversing with her as a possible danger. Whenever you really like someone, you additionally will more often than not feel desirous over the smallest male-female connections that that individual has with others. You become effectively envious assuming the individual whom you like discussions to the individual of the contrary orientation, effectively mixing up that individual to be somebody who is attempting to prevail upon your crush.

•••

•••

•••

•••

•••

You will more often than not take a gander at her 11/10 times with a consistent anxiety toward getting found out.Having a pound causes you to feel butterflies in your stomach at whatever point you see them. You feel a feeling of joy when you are around them and giggle by any stretch of the imagination of their jokes despite the fact that some of them are awful. You likewise will generally fit towards on the positive side of them that you see now and let everyone how great they are know if they were your accomplice. With the negatives, you overlook them, and avoid on to existence without initial reasoning through the warnings shown and the alerts uncovered.

Also, you have this yearning for this unique individual whom you like.

You begin adjusting your perspectives, your activities, your words, and so on to establish a decent connection with them. You begin settling on choices that could attract you nearer to your crush and may concoct clever reasons to be close to them. You need to be close to them since they cause you to feel far better within. They rouse you to do things you wouldn't ordinarily do. You stay since they're there, you go in light of the fact that they left.

Personally, when I have a crush, I experience butterflies in my stomach yet my face is nonpartisan. I look uninterested yet I express all the conceivable not-really clear signs that I like you.

Do you recollect your first crush? Do you recollect the urge it took to converse with them? That strained climate, that heartbeat, golly! That made us every one of the awkward minimal modest child, yet at the same time it was charming. You should think how this is satisfying us? How is this something we ought to consider motivation to grin? Obviously it is one of the greatest I would agree,

• • •

• • •

• • •

reason that brought a, no, bunches of grin on our countenances.

As I told you before, I contemplated in three schools, moved to one and afterward another. So I sort of have more pounds, Sometimes I can't help thinking about the fact that I was so moronic to make that individual my crush, as genuinely. Be that as it may, don't bother, I was a child in those days and everything felt charming. At any point got smash on your instructor? Indeed we as a whole did. Particularly the English one.

The entire class used to have a pound for her, including young ladies. OK perhaps! We used to respect the manner in which she talks, her profluent jargon used to make us the entire fall for herself and the manner in which she used to really focus on each youngster in the class, golly our liquefying point. Dislike the P.E educator who just used to set up a pencil between our fingers and press it with his full power. Ugh, that harms a ton. At any rate, Every time somebody who is named as a pound in our lives used to enter in the study hall, everything felt so unique.

Basically, seeing them and their face fulfills you such that you go off the deep end about what their life is like. You get truly inquisitive as well as watching your own behavior, and so forth you treat them contrastingly on the grounds that they caused you to feel unique. They're different on the grounds that they have a ton of characteristics that you like in an individual that it is difficult to decline a deal/solicitation to follow through with something or head off to some place with them.

Having a crush makes your brain wired and focused on them the entire day when you see them or know their presence. You are cognizant that they are there and act distinctively when they are near, and so on and get turned on by the positive things that they do.

• • •

• • •

It is difficult to get switched off except if assuming that individual does something terrible to you straightforwardly, harms your companions, and so on You begin tuning in with their sentiments and furthermore begin to track down similitudes with them, wanting to ignite up a wonderful discussion with them where you don't on the grounds that there are questions in your mind that pull you back.

You have a small scale fit of anxiety each time they approach, or collaborate with you, you can't quit contemplating them. This is odd, yet at a certain point, you'll attempt to find their folks or them simply overall on Facebook or Instagram. You'll have no less than 2-3 humiliating minutes with them, and your psyche generally takes you back to think about it consistently.

You'll continuously consider what they'll think while picking an outfit, your hair, your stench , and so on Assuming you notice them taking a gander at you for somewhere around at least 2 seconds, you'll lose it the subsequent you're everything alone. You'll discover yourself looking into "how to make your crush like you" recordings on YouTube at 4 AM. On the off chance that you believe that they aren't seeing or liking you enough, you'll successfully change your appearance to make them search for close to a second.

That positive energy they carried with themselves was used to enlighten the whole class and our hearts. That little part of your life made you grin, giving you the motivation to grin. Never missing the school or going to the class rather than bunk just to be close to them welcomed a grin on your countenances. Regardless of whether it's another person's crush, we get delighted from prodding them.

• • •

• • •

• • •

• • •

At any point pondered that our supposed "crushes", are showing us a significant life illustration. "To let go".

To let go in life is one of the significant standards to carry on with a superior life. Allow me to clarify this by taking this smash section, you succumb to somebody you get drawn to, you ponder them to an extreme,

they are generally at the forefront of your thoughts.

Assuming the individual you're crushin' on has communicated that they're not keen on you similarly, then, at that point, let it go. The most horrendously terrible thing you can do now is develop bogus expectation that something might in any case occur. Acknowledge that both of you may very well be made to be companions and perceive that you merit somebody who realizes they like you for you! You shouldn't need to do any persuading.

Since the individual you like would rather avoid like you, it doesn't mean you need to thoroughly dispense with them from your life. As a matter of fact, assuming you folks began as companions, there's definitely not an obvious explanation for why you shouldn't attempt to keep a fellowship. You don't need to be best pals, yet this individual clearly implied or implies a great deal to you, so be caring and understanding and give your all to be well disposed. They'll cherish that you're being the greater individual.

Think about what, as banality as it might sound, it's actually their misfortune, not yours. You as of now have so much going for you, so rather than allowing your pity to bamboozle you, center around your astounding characteristics in general and do exercises that cause you to feel blissful and engaged. Go on a run, practice your

• • •

• • •

• • •

leisure activity or call a companion. You are your main need the present moment, and that is really magnificent.

To let go you should observe the accompanying guidelines.

Make a positive mantra to counter the positive considerations

How you talk or how you manage yourself after such

occurrences can determine if you're pushing ahead or you're recently stuck. The first and the main individual you've to comfort is you, you need to propel yourself without fail, rather than asking yourself, " I can't really accept that this happened to me " inspire yourself by saying " I am lucky to have the option to observe another way throughout everyday life, that is great for me ".

• • •

• • •

Actual distance

It's difficult to avoid somebody who is making you upset. We get so associated that is all there is to it somewhat unimaginable. Yet, you can do anything. Making an actual distance can help us in pushing ahead in this way keeping away from us to be stuck. It's more straightforward to acknowledge that you are enough for yourself now of life.

• • •

• • •

Go about your own responsibilities

Focusing in on yourself is significant. You need to settle on the decision to address the hurt that you've encountered. At the point when you ponder an individual who caused you torment, take yourself back to the present. Then, at

• • •

• • •

that point, center around something that you're appreciative for.

• • •

Be delicate with yourself

In the event that your first reaction to not having the option to relinquish what is going on is to condemn yourself, now is the ideal time to offer yourself a few grace and sympathy. Try not to get brutal on yourself, lamenting on things that weren't in your grasp. Acknowledge reality and be delicate with yourself. Life is a thrill ride of high points and low points, generally downs I generally say. You'll always be there with yourselves, from birth to no end, so support yourself in each part of life.

• • •

• • •

• • •

• • •

• • •

• • •

• • •

• • •

• • •

• • •

• • •

THE PARTNER

Here comes the most fragile and significant piece of our lives. I would agree for the greater part of us it's likewise an astonishing one. A large numbers of us need to live their lives uninhibitedly, they don't need it to be connected with somebody or in their words, "chained to somebody". But that is where they are exacerbating it for themselves, might be not in a present moment but rather in a long haul unquestionably. When you get married a new soul is connected to you, a new life is bonded with you. Who's going to stay with you till your last breadth, firstly let's pray for everyone that there soul mate lasts with them till their last moments? Remember when we were children, the feeling of someone getting married brings so joy in us, that we start making scenarios of our marriage. We start imagining our soul mate even though we'll meet him/her maybe years later.

• • •

A soul mate is a person with whom one has a feeling of deep or natural affinity. This may involve similarity, love, romance, platonic relationships, comfort, intimacy, spirituality, compatibility and trust. On average, husbands and wives are healthier, happier and enjoy longer lives than those who are not married. In current usage, "soul mate" usually refers to a romantic or platonic partner, with the implication of an exclusive lifelong bond. It commonly holds the connotation of being the strongest bond with another person that one can achieve. It is commonly accepted that one will feel 'complete' once they have found their soul mate, as it is partially in the perceived definition that two souls are meant to unite. There's a massive increase in your reasons to smile when

• • •

• • •

• • •

you find your soul mate. You can now move on with your life since you found one of the treasures you were looking for! It can be really nice to find your partner in crime early on so that you don't have to waste years of your life in potential heartache and loneliness.

Someone other than you parents to support you in your personal goals and dreams. You are more likely to achieve your goals when you verbalize them to other people. A shared sense of meaning and purpose in life. Healthy couples create meaning together whether that's sharing pursuits, contributing to a community together, practicing religion together, etc. Less stress. Healthy couples are able to provide comfort for one another and to support one another in the face of stress. The opportunity to care for someone else. Caring for others is shown to have positive health benefits. Someone to account for your life. Your partner is a witness to who you are and what you do. Your life is important to your partner and matters to them.

Emotional support. Your partner validates your reality and helps you make sense of your experiences. Your partner usually knows you better than anyone else. They know when you're feeling good and when you're feeling low–sometimes just by the way you walk or the tone of your voice. If you had a horrible day at work, they can be a sounding board, offer support, and help you decompress. There are many reasons for your partner to bring a smile on your face. I'm not married yet, so all this is just a guess and life lessons from someone who is already married. We all face difficulties in our lives, and it's okay to fail at some, By having a great partner it makes all these times a lot easier to go through.

No marriage is happy all of the time. "Like all relationships, there are ups and downs," But when you do fight, happy marriages listen to each other's point of view, recognize when the argument is going off the rails, and make the

• • •

• • •

necessary repairs, she says. In fact based on a research, some of the happiest couples she has worked with “have weathered hard times.

”So if you and your spouse sometimes argue, or are going through a rough patch, this does not necessarily mean you are in an unhappy marriage. In fact, it probably means you’re normal.

Assuming that you depend on your life partner to satisfy you, it can prompt an over-subordinate relationship where you are not developing as people. All things considered, couples in solid connections ought to "supplement," not "complete" each other, she says. "We ought to be secure, mature, and entire in ourselves while being available to the next individual." So ensure you support your own advantages and wants take a class you’re keen on, make arrangements with companions as opposed to trusting that your life partner will make up for in the shortfall. furthermore, will turn into reason to clear out a grin from your face.

While it’s critical to not completely rely upon your accomplice to keep a cheerful marriage, it’s likewise important to share normal encounters. "Infusing new exercises and interests into your relationship can reinforce the bond,”.

Life is upsetting, so it helps assuming you can observe gentility in any event, when you’re in a mess. "Ordinarily a few has humor, it implies they have viewpoint," couples observe giggling in both great and terrible times. In blissful relationships have a straightforwardness around one another.

Whether it’s through minimal inside jokes, a senseless startling text, or even watching your cherished

• • •

• • •

• • •

• • •

satire together, interfacing with your life partner with chuckling can build your bond, and will without a doubt carry many motivations to remain blissful.

At the point when you're with somebody constantly, it's not difficult to underestimate them, yet you should verbally communicate your appreciation consistently. Whether you're pointing out good something insightful they've done, or telling them something you like about them, We all need to feel appreciated and supported for the things we are doing well. For instance, on the off chance that your companion makes you tea toward the beginning of the day, let them know it began your day happily. In the event that we don't feel esteemed we might become angry and become separated.

Everybody commits errors. Your partner might offend you or accomplish something that disturbs you, and that might drive you crazy, even angry. In any case, it's critical to manage your sentiments, let them go, and continue on. try not to continue to raise the past.

Make sure to stay focused on your partner, your family, and the existence that you have fabricated together. Support each other sincerely and in ordinary ways. You, your partnet, and your relationship might develop and change with time, yet these thoughts can assist your marriage with remaining effective throughout the long term.

Focus on seemingly insignificant details, make your bond more grounded and partake in the satisfaction with one another. Eventually giving out more joy sharing one another's.

CHAPTER IV

SCIENCE BEHIND YOUR HAPPINESS

When was the last time you felt ridiculously blissful or happy i would say? What causes bliss like that? What's more, what satisfies a few of us practically constantly, while others fight with issues like misery and struggle feeling blissful? What substance fulfills you?

It isn't only one compound in a specific sum that satisfies us. The study of satisfaction lets us know that neurological synthetic substances like dopamine and serotonin differ from one individual to another, making them feel pretty much cheerful throughout everyday life. Yet, does dopamine fulfill you? Does serotonin satisfy you? The response is that these are factors in our general prosperity, however they're not by any means the only thing you should be cheerful.

Joy relies upon numerous things. Your state changes relying upon how you respond to changes in your vocation, marriage, individual life and funds. Joy can likewise be expected to a limited extent to rewarding individuals and local area around you, taking on a development attitude during testing times and gaining ground throughout everyday life. We are regularly more in charge of our bliss than we might suspect - we can sort out what causes satisfaction, then, at that point, develop it

• • •

• • •

• • •

• • •

• • •

through a bunch of procedures and practices that anybody can rehearse.

• • •

What chemically makes you happy?

People are wired to look for delight and keep away from torment; we look to make due throughout everyday life, except to encounter what satisfies us. Our cerebrum science is intended to help these endeavors by delivering synthetics into our mind and body that cause us to feel better. There are various synapses, or substances delivered by nerve strands, that influence joy. In spite of the fact that there are many that cause us to feel euphoric, at the present time we'll zero in on four: serotonin, dopamine, oxytocin and endorphins.

• • •

• • •

SEROTONIN

Serotonin is a synapse that is made in the cerebrum as well as in the digestive organs. When delivered, it's circled in the blood and all through the focal sensory system. While there is anything but a solitary solution to what substance satisfies you, serotonin is a fundamental piece of the riddle. A few researchers even allude to serotonin as the "satisfaction synthetic," on the grounds that higher serotonin levels increment sensations of prosperity, certainty and having a place.

People are social creatures, and being around others causes joy for a significant number of us. There's a logical justification behind that: Serotonin is all the more free-streaming when you feel significant or esteemed by people around you. While you're

• • •

• • •

encountering serotonin bliss, it requires no work to feel euphoric –

it simply appears to happen normally or in other words it is more free-flowing when you feel important or valued by those around you. it takes no effort to feel joyful – it just seems to happen naturally

Individuals who are determined to have sorrow regularly have low degrees of serotonin accessible, though individuals with high serotonin frequently report being more joyful. Individuals with higher serotonin levels likewise show more significant levels of confidence and make some more straightforward memories taking care of dismissal.

Serotonin is additionally connected to assimilation, blood coagulating and bone thickness, and lopsidedness can create both mental and actual issues. Absence of serotonin can cause issues with solid discharges, queasiness and rest designs. It might influence your capacity to recuperate wounds by thickening blood. Then again, a lot of serotonin might assume a part in osteoporosis and can really lessen your charisma.

So does serotonin makes you happy? The short response is yes - and you don't need to depend on your regular serotonin levels. Cuddling with your partner, aerobic exercise, getting out in the sunshine, getting a massage and even visualizing something that makes you happy can all increase serotonin levels.

• • •

• • •

• • •

• • •

• • •

• • •

DOPAMINE

Does dopamine satisfy you?

Dopamine is one more synapse made in the cerebrum and conveyed through different pathways to influence basic physical processes like pulse, vein and kidney work, sickness, heaving and even torment. Yet, does dopamine fulfill you? Truth be told, it is maybe generally renowned for its part in the study of joy.

Your body discharges dopamine as a feature of the award framework - after sex or a decent supper, or when you've arrived at an objective. That is the reason it's known as the "reward particle." thusly, it assumes a part in how rapidly and productively you finish things. Your body knows that assuming it accomplishes a goal, your brain will flood the body with dopamine making you feel blissful and satisfied.

This isn't simply valid for accomplishing major objectives. In any event, when you achieve a little assignment, your dopamine levels will increment. Dopamine satisfaction feels fortifying and empowering. Individuals with low degrees of dopamine could encounter misery or other temperament problems and can experience difficulty remaining focused and staying centered.

Dopamine is one more crucial solution to what synthetic satisfies you - and like serotonin, you can expand its levels normally. Practice has an influence again here, as well as staying away from handled food varieties, sugar and caffeine. However, the most effective way to keep dopamine levels high? Get a decent night's rest.

• • •

• • •

• • •

• • •

OXYTOCIN

Have you at any point felt like you simply required an embrace, a hug? That might have been your mind looking

for oxytocin. The cerebrum delivers this synapse during actual contact and in any event, when you play out a good thought. Oxytocin is essential to parent-kid holding, labor and breastfeeding. As such a significant piece of the reinforcements of life, it's nothing unexpected this chemical keeps on influencing our bliss well into adulthood.

While dopamine gives us a "hit" of joy, oxytocin plays a drawn out job, giving sensations of quiet, wellbeing and trust. It assists us with making profound companionships, fall head over heels and construct energetic connections. Whenever you give a companion an embrace, snuggle with your accomplice or participate in closeness, oxytocin benefits both you and your accomplice.

Oxytocin can likewise assist with interceding the more habit-forming characteristics of "effective" dopamine, helps our invulnerable frameworks, further develops critical thinking abilities and diminishes pressure. Studies are continuous into its consequences for points as different as wound recuperating, dependence and cerebrum injury.

While understanding oxytocin is only one piece of knowing what synthetic satisfies you, it's particularly critical to long haul bliss and satisfaction throughout everyday life. What's more, as indicated by the study of satisfaction, expanding your levels of this chemical is pretty much as simple as giving somebody an embrace, a hug.

• • •

• • •

• • •

• • •

CORTISOL: THE ENEMY OF WHAT MAKES US HAPPY

While there are natural biological conditions that decline the levels of these synthetic substances, they are regularly adjusted in the people who eat nutritious weight control plans, get a lot of activity and deal with their feelings of anxiety really. Notwithstanding, for the people who lead undesirable ways of life or allowed pressure to assume control north of, a destructive synthetic called cortisol can be delivered and repress the synthetic compounds that satisfy us.

Cortisol is a chemical made by the body's adrenal organs. In typical sums, it lessens irritation in the body and manages pulse, blood glucose and rest. It's additionally the body's fundamental pressure chemical and is generally popular for actuating the "instinctive" reaction.

While you're living in a condition of steady pressure, cortisol becomes raised. This state not just diminishes our bliss, it additionally adversely impacts memory and concentration, can prompt weight gain and can effect sly affect our significant organs and resistant framework.

Does dopamine satisfy you? Sure. Serotonin does, as well. However, you can't carry on with life pondering just what synthetic fulfills you. You wouldn't need a mind loaded up with just the "cheerful" synapses and none of the others. Your body needs both. Because in the end, what causes happiness comes down to one word which is "balance".

• • •

• • •

• • •

• • •

• • •

STRATEGIES FOR BALANCE IN THE BRAIN

You could imagine that in light of the fact that your mind is wired a specific way that there's no way around your ordinary joy. All things considered, a portion of this is hereditary, isn't that so? While it is actually the case that your cerebrum science is impacted by your science, the study of bliss shows that you have the ability to change your contemplations. On the off chance that the accompanying procedures don't work and you are encountering a downturn you can't shake, look for professional assistance.

• • •

1. MOVE YOUR BODY

Get up and continue consistently for at minimum an hour to deliver endorphins and lift your mind-set.

• • •

2. PRACTICE GRATITUDE

You can likewise rehearse appreciation routinely by writing in a diary, thinking deeply about every one of the beneficial things in your day to day existence or tracking down ways of showing appreciation to those near you.

• • •

3. FEED YOUR MIND

Try to take care of your psyche with nutritious data like self-improvement guides, fascinating memoirs or inspirational books.

• • •

4. Encircle YOURSELF WITH SUPPORT

At long last, encircle yourself with the individuals who are good and strong will animate the arrival of "feel better" cerebrum synthetic substances and assist you with

staying in a pinnacle state. Nobody feels blissful without fail, yet the study of satisfaction shows us that there are things we can do to support our temperament. In any event, when you face a test, you can figure out how to acknowledge and gain from it. By making close friendly associations and gaining ground throughout everyday life, you have the capacity to reevaluate your outlook and make a pattern of bliss. While synapses absolutely influence your state, as Tony Robbins says, "Progress equals happiness."

I Thank to Tony Robbins (an American author) for an impeccable data on the science behind satisfaction.

CHAPTER V

THE PATH OF PRAYING

Each Human being on this planet whether he is rich or poor, dark or white, common or bourgeoisie, king or beggar, Muslim or non-Muslim, is looking for harmony. The significant component which a human requirements the most for living is mental harmony.

Internal harmony lies in two significant things: in serving the mankind and in the recognition of Allah. Islam has placed incredible accentuation on both of these things. That wouldn't be wrong to say that Islam is the religion of harmony and serenity. Islamic lessons lead to the internal harmony on the off chance that individuals follow them according to the direction of Quran and Sunnah. As Allah says in Surah "O People of the Scripture, there has come to you Our Messenger clarifying to you a lot of what you used to hide of the Scripture and disregarding a lot. There has come to you from Allah a light and an unmistakable Book. By which Allah directs the individuals who seek after His pleasure to the methods of harmony and exposes them out from dimness, by His authorization, and guides them to a straight way".

The above refrains express that we have the sacred writing as Quran which is the finished manual, and we have the way of life of Prophet Mohammad (p.b.u.h) to know the correct approach to everyday life. In religion Islam, Muslims have been directed in their all social statuses by referencing the advantages and disadvantages of each and everything. Presently it depends on individuals

• • •

• • •

• • •

that on the off chance that they are concentrating on the Islam or not to get the right ways of life which at last

advantage the personalities with harmony and serenity.

Numerous analysts and behaviorists contend that by the day's end the best human drive is mental harmony. Islam is the way to harmony and peacefulness. In Islam it begins with the most fundamental thing for example welcoming among Muslims; Muslims are endorsed to welcome each other at whatever point they meet, which is a type of good signal. In the present life which is so engaged with online media, do we truly have the change to welcome somebody face to face? Another explanation which is affecting our psychological harmony. An average number of individuals would rather not welcome another on the grounds that they are not doing as such. We foster a type of self-image, which results into an undesirable attitude. Considering this hello signal we can acquire a major transform us, at last making a bye to our self-ego.

Have you at any point asked? Whoever god you put stock in, by for me there's just god, and we simply have given various names or you can say these supposed " religion master" have begun a business out of it, it's a totally different point or a book I can say, so leave it here.

Do you recollect when we you were a child , you used to go to get toys, or to get passing marks, " god I need that new hot wheels set" , "god I'll study next time I guarantee give me good grades once", we as a whole use to do as such. Well that is something else in the event that your petition gets replied or not, however the fulfillment or you can say the psychological harmony you accomplish in the wake of letting you know individual issues to somebody, the god. You accept that yes there is somebody who's paying attention to you, you're not apprehensive, you

• • •

• • •

were before you supplicated, you were stressed like heck, you were misrepresenting yet presently it's gone. It's

tranquility all over, you're quiet.

Asking and paying attention to the responses God provides you can assist you with better getting your motivation throughout

everyday life. God will assist you with understanding the reason why you are here and how you might get back to live with Him after this life.

Whenever you secretly implore God, you can manage serious decisions in your life. God generally tunes in and regularly gives the particular responses and direction we look for. In any event, when He decides not to answer right away or in the manner we could have trusted, supplication itself is a method for discovering a true sense of reconciliation.

All through the sacred texts, we see numerous instances of the Lord working supernatural occurrences as a response to supplication. In Old Testament times, the prophet Daniel was tossed into a lions' nook since he wouldn't quit asking. At the point when he petitioned God in the lions' den, heavenly messengers showed up and shut the mouths of the lions. Through every day petition, you can likewise encounter individual miracles such as recuperating, harmony, and pardon for sins.

There is anything but a solitary person on earth who doesn't go through his portion of difficulties bound for him. These accounts are intended to guide and assist us with defeating any difficulties we face. Indeed, even the prophets were tried with the deficiency of friends and family, abundance, and wellbeing.

• • •

• • •

• • •

• • •

Prophet Yusuf was a descendant of an ancestry of Prophets. He was the child of Prophet Yaqub, grandson of Prophet Ishaq, and the extraordinary grandson of Prophet Ibrahim (May Allah's approval accompany them all).

Prophet Yusuf consumed the vast majority of his time on earth getting through plans by individuals nearest to him. His envious siblings plotted to kill him however rather left him in a well, he was then gotten by a voyaging troop and sold in the slave market. He was purchased by a man who raised him like his own child. His confidence was tried once more when the King's better half attempted to lure him yet her arrangement was thwarted and he was shipped off jail for a long time. Later delivered and was assigned on a significant position, working close by.

• • •

The story of prophet Yusuf gave us numerous life illustrations, "Everybody Deserves To Be Treated Kindly" When Prophet Yusuf was in jail, he managed the detainees with the greatest amount of graciousness. He addressed them about Allah SWT. Continuously have confidence in the positive qualities in an individual, his transgressions are awful it doesn't make the person awful in general. Figure out how to detest the wrongdoing not the heathen. Since, in such a case that Allah wills he can be directed to the correct way. Shaitan is on a consistent mission to misinform individuals, today we disdain an individual on account of a specific awful deed, perhaps tomorrow Allah denies that wrongdoing can turn into a piece of our life as well.

• • •

"Forgive"

Whenever Prophet Yusuf given the place of Treasurer, he encountered his siblings. His siblings were exceptionally humiliated and felt regret. Rather than boasting, he excused them.

Figure out how to excuse, yes our confidence isn't unreasonably solid, it harms frightfully when somebody nearest to us is the reason for our aggravation. We want to get payback, yet recall that Allah SWT does the best equity, pass on it to him, and even better pardon and given up. It will just raise and make us more noteworthy before Allah.

• • •

"Have tolerance"

Whenever Prophet Yusuf's siblings returned without him, Prophet Yaqub was troubled however he showed restraint. At the point when life presents any obstructions tolerance and confidence in Allah SWT is the main thing that can help us through. Impediments are a piece of life, it is to perceive the way that we respond whether we are appreciative or grumble.

At the point when episodes unfurl in our lives, they could appear to be troublesome however what is to come nobody knows, and for better or for more regrettable that is the thing is bound and best for us. This is what the account of Prophet Yusuf shows us, regardless of whether individuals nearest to you conflict with you, as long as your confidence in Allah is solid, He will open entryways for you in your most obscure minutes.

CHAPTER VI

GIVE SHIT A LITTLE

Giving shit on generally everything going around is a routine group are acquiring nowadays. They act over the top with things, Alright We make too much of things, I'm making an effort not to give shit about things that make me discouraged. Also, I surmise everybody is attempting. It has turned into a propensity, to encircle ourselves with something that can constantly wreck your psyche and not giving now is the ideal time to unwind. From " damn, I didn't awaken at the alert" to " I bombed again ".

Everything we do is to give shit. Giving shit can be of two kinds, one where the reason is great for the wellbeing, beneficient for us, can help us in improving our lives. Second is the one which controls our brain, which draws out the most exceedingly awful from us, which can make us discouraged. This one is your foe, we need to dispose of this.

" With each stress we take, there's a decrement in our grins" . We need to separate which one is the great crap and which isn't. Like for instance, a kid fizzled in a pre test, he makes too much of that crap that he makes himself debilitated, and revile himself for not ready to pass, despite the fact that the last tests of the year are planned at this point.

This is the shit we ought to stay away from in our lives. It's alright to flop once in a while to rise. However, approaching that fall in a serious way, will make it hard for you to rise.

• • •

• • •

• • •

Truly everybody cares a whole lot about something. Cash, Power, Sex, Status. No difference either way. Indeed, even individuals you consider not caring a lot like the criminals, ISIS, Pablo Escobar, and so forth, all gave loads of shits, perhaps not about exactly the same things that you or I do, however they did. Everybody does.

It's incomprehensible not to care a lot about anything, nor is simply attractive. Truth be told, it's essential to care now and then, If you don't care a whole lot working, you'll get terminated

On the off chance that you don't care a whole lot in business, you'll before long be bankrupt. On the off chance that you don't care a whole lot about your companions, you before long will not have any companions. Giving shit a little have many benefits. You at last see that anything that's happening in someone else's psyche shouldn't affect your choices at any rate.

The internal voice in your mind is the main assessment that really matters and when you at last understand that idea your considerations will change in a positive manner. You used to continually stress over individuals' opinion on you. Your appearance, your decisions, your fantasies, your interests, your leisure activities, anything that it could be. You at last comprehend that the main individual that genuinely has something to do with your life is you.

You begin giving your energy towards your inclinations and individuals that really matter. Quit focusing on harmful individuals and dull connections that used to consume your contemplations. You never again need someone else's endorsement to be content. Assuming you enjoy a leisure activity you love, seek after it with great enthusiasm. You're not worried what any other individual is doing and you've figured out how to focus on the spot you're

• • •

• • •

• • •

possessing, and individuals you're with at each given second. You know how to completely be available and relinquished superfluous things that have consumed space in your brain for so long.

You quit attempting to substantiate yourself. Quit sitting around idly on molding or changing individuals' view of you. Rather than attempting to acquire somebody's regard and consideration, you know how to do those things for yourself. Assuming somebody can't understand what you offer of real value, distance yourself from that individual. You don't have to encircle yourself with cause you to feel like you want to substantiate yourself. Since to be absolutely fair, you truly don't.

You begin to do things you really need to do, not things you simply figure you ought to do. At the point when you quit focusing on others' thought process of you begin to see life from a previously unheard-of viewpoint. You begin living for yourself as opposed to agonizing over what others anticipate from you. You do things since you need to do them, rather than destroying them dislike of a response from others.

You settle on choices in light of what you need, not in view of how you will appear to other people. You used to stress over what your choices would mean for individuals around you. What might they think assuming I did that? Could that resentful them? Presently, you're ready to settle on valuable choices for you without culpability being a component.

In the event that somebody would rather avoid a choice you make, that is their concern, not yours-and you at long last perceive that. It makes life a great deal more charming when you care about what you think and not what every other person thinks. You don't have to account for yourself any longer. On the off chance that you would rather not go

• • •

• • •

out to a bar on Friday night, essentially say "no" without wanting to legitimize why. Grapple with the way that not every person will continuously concur with the choices you make.

In any case, insofar as you're content with those choices it doesn't make any difference what any other person thinks. Life is significantly simpler and much more joyful when the main individual you owe a clarification to is yourself. You have full authorization to settle on options without accounting for yourself.

You are at this point not a captive to unimportant judgment from others.

Yann Girard is an Author, I read a blog of him and got it truly impacted by it from a decent perspective. He said, Most of us simply aren't Mark Zuckerberg or Steve Jobs or Elon Musk and that is thoroughly fine. Or on the other hand perhaps you are. I don't have any acquaintance with you. In any case, I think for a large portion of us it's a way better plan to simply practice a piece in the nursery on that trampoline prior to leaping off that bluff. To make many little wagers. Prior to making that immense bet. Rather than leaping off the precipice immediately. What's more, whenever you've dominated that one thing you can happen to the following thing. One stage at a time.And I firmly accept that you shouldn't think often about all of this stuff by the same token. The one thing you ought to truly think often about however, the one thing that truly matters is that you do your thing. Furthermore, act naturally. Furthermore, begin doing the things that will assist you with carrying on with the everyday routine you generally needed to experience. Regardless of what.And in the event that you don't have the foggiest idea what these things are, then, at that point, reconsider. You likely know the exact thing those things are.

• • •

• • •

• • •

It's typically the things you've been attempting to overlook. The entire time. These are typically the things you ought to do. The things you were fleeing from. The things you realize where it counts you ought to do however were excessively scared of.

In any case, without leaping off a precipice. Without committing suicide. Kindly, don't off yourself. The world necessities you. The world necessities to hear your story. So show restraint. What's more, begin investing the effort. What's more, consistently attempt to get back up once more. Furthermore, go mindfully. Try not to go thirty stages all at once in light of the fact that the main thing that will happen is that you will stagger and fall. Go with care all things considered. Since getting back up again in the wake of tumbling down a precipice after you've avoided 30 stages is beyond difficult. Look. Life is only a game. Also, we'll be dead toward the finish of it at any rate. So you should attempt to live however long you can. Furthermore, attempt to not off yourself while simultaneously you should attempt to not live in dread all

the time. I attempt to continually advise myself that I will not have the option to get out alive of this thing at any rate. And afterward I attempt to advise myself that I would rather not spend my final gasps thinking "what might have occurred assuming I did... "And all things considered, I take care of business. Regardless. However, consistently attempt to recall that parachute story. Attempt to abstain from doing everything inept. Attempt to not off yourself. Furthermore, go one stage at a time. Everything he said is on point.

The expression "That we as a whole will bite the dust eventually" is frightening however that is the reality of life. We are so impacted by this performing various tasks, that we give a great deal of crap about what's circumventing

• • •

• • •

us. Just take Mark Zuckerberg for instance, he's occupied in his social techniques making new internet peculiarities, yet he is bound to this one work. If we get some information about how to set the lightning for a film scene, conceivable outcomes are he could don't have the foggiest idea. Since he's engaged to a certain something, or one thing at a time.Giving way many craps can make a difficult issue our wellbeing.

• • •

• • •

• • •

• • •

• • •

• • •

• • •

• • •

• • •

• • •

• • •

• • •

• • •

• • •

WHY LIVING IN THE PRESENT IS MORE IMPORTANT

We as a whole longing veritable bliss, and to show this satisfaction we need to live by and by. An excess of spotlight on the future regularly prompts pressure and negative reasoning. Anticipating what's to come is great to stay away from disappointments, monetary issues, choices prompting more terrible circumstances. We should expand why living in the present is more significant for us.

"The secret of health for both mind and body is not to mourn for the past, worry about the future, or anticipate troubles, but to live in the present moment wisely and earnestly." -Buddha

The present moment is the only moment you have control over right now

Regardless of the amount you plan you never know without a doubt the way in which life will work out. The possibly time you will know is the point at which you are at that time.

• • •

The second you experience right presently is the main second you have some control over. You can decide to partake in the second or you can decide to severely dislike the occasion. You can likewise decide to overlook the second totally and squander it away, however in any case, the current second is yours to control.

Arranging won't remove you from the present. It could assist you with achieving your objectives yet it won't work on your personal satisfaction for the current second. Arranging won't promise you an ideal result for the future so why not acknowledge what you have some control over at this point?

• • •

• • •

• • •

• • •

• • •

Every second is a gift

There is no assurance on the quantity of minutes you will get to encounter. This is critical to understand. Nobody knows when the following snapshot of their life will be detracted from them. Your next second isn't ensured, so why not exploit the one you are ready?

• • •

You can't live with this special point of view assuming that you are continually making arrangements for the following phase of your life. You can encounter this get-up-and-go on the off chance that you are living right now. It might even sound silly and ridiculous, yet it appears to be legit.

• • •

Try not to underestimate minutes. Plan when it is essential however not to the detriment of you partaking in the current second. As the old banality expresses that life is short, so you appreciate it while you can.

• • •

• • •

• • •

Being available is an incredible pressure minimizer

Contemplating the future, and the past, are regularly reasons for pressure. Despite the fact that some pressure can be gainful, the pressure caused from not living at the time can be adverse to one's psychological, physical, and passionate wellbeing.

• • •

• • •

Over-arranging can prompt pointless pressure while the arranging keeps you from living at the time. Fortify your everyday routine with present experiencing procedures that will empower you to remain more centered around every second.

• • •

You presumably don't have the advantage of reflecting five hours every day and not setting some sort of arrangement for your future, yet carrying out little changes into your life should assist with lessening pressure.

• • •

See when your brain starts to zero in on the future rather than the current second you are encountering. Inquire as to whether this point of view is important. Basic mindfulness and acknowledgment of your contemplations will help you in being more present.

• • •

• • •

Designs frequently don't show themselves the manner in which you need or anticipate.

This is a reality regardless of whether you need to trust it. How frequently have you taken a stab at arranging something however it simply didn't work out the manner in which you need? How could you respond? Did you become disturbed or did you handle what is going on with acknowledgment and understanding Whenever I plan something generally it ends up being unique. I, at the end of the day, plan a ton, I make situations in a real sense.

• • •

In any case, when the result emerges to be different it harms. My own recommendation is attempt less to consider what's to come, it won't be the specific the way that you anticipated.

Plans fall flat. As an individual from a defective animal categories, you bomb frequently. It is a piece of life.

• • •

Endeavoring to anticipate each progression of your life isn't just incomprehensible however it is presumably not beneficial for you. The more you plan, the more probable you are to become aggravated or disturbed when those plans don't come into realization. Bringing about influencing your wellbeing.

• • •

I'm not recommending you shouldn't design with the demeanor that the arrangement will fall flat, yet I am suggesting that you let life play its course and simply be. Remain positive with whats coming.

Feel free to make arrangements in the event that that is useful for you however don't neglect to focus on the current second. On the off chance that your arrangements don't work out the manner in which you need, then essentially attempt to acknowledge it.

CHAPTER VII

The Books Around The World

The Subtle Art of Mark Manson

Who is more relatable in dealing with rejections or giving way many f**k, other than Mark Manson? You mustn't have heard his name yet the name of his book "The Subtle Art of Not Giving A F**k " This books expresses that, Observing something significant and significant in your life is the most useful utilization of your time and energy. This is valid on the grounds that each life has issues related with it and observing importance in your life will assist you with supporting the work expected to defeat the specific issues you face. Accordingly, we can say that the way to carrying on with a decent life isn't caring a lot about more things, things that can shake our inward harmony, things that can remove our grins, yet rather, caring just about the things that line up with your own values.

Things that really imply something to you, something which might sting in brief time frame of period however is good for a long term. We have such a lot of fucking stuff that we don't have any idea what to care a whole lot about any longer. You want to track down what to care a lot about. You should care a lot about something.

• • •

• • •

Understanding your own qualities is the main test we as a whole face to lead a superior, more joyful life.

"Personal growth" is truly about: focusing on better qualities, picking better things to care a whole lot about. Deciding to say no, to diminish choices, and live with less, can prompt a more joyful life. What is it that you truly desire? At the end of the day, what's your definitive objective - the accomplishment you need to be composed on your tombstone?

It's not a simple inquiry to respond to, right? Indeed, large numbers of us will guarantee that we need bliss, a caring family and a task we appreciate, however these are unclear aspirations. Furthermore unclear desires are hazardous on the grounds that they won't push you to make progress toward progress.

Tragically, to go anyplace throughout everyday life, you'll need to battle. Accomplishing your objectives will require difficult work and a lot of steadiness; it's reliable that there will be misfortunes and difficulties on the way. Dealing with something that fulfills you implies you'll not exclusively be determined by the consistent fight; you'll develop to cherish it.

• • •

• • •

The Rudest Boy Shwetabh Gangwar

I generally read books that impact my conduct. Last year I read this person's "The Rudest Book Ever", and I should say that it affected my conduct in a positive manner. The book is however rudest as its title seems to be. The book is an assortment of points of view and thoughts on liberating your psyche from all horse crap. The reality of life you would seldom hear from guardians, companions, society, or the web.

Shwetabh has conclusions as everybody on the planet will in general have. Each snippet of data accessible now is

only the result of somebody's thoughts and considerations. You can have your own perspectives and thoughts regarding all that you can concoct. You, yourself, and doing your thought process is the best matter most than anything more. All the other things are auxiliary.

The world doesn't give a flying fuck about you. You are 100 percent all alone. Never expect a supernatural occurrence or an enchanted pill to fix any of your concerns.

No one wants to think about it. No one truly minds except if they have a rationale to do as such. No one ponders you when nearly everybody is narcissistic inside themselves. An individual's gentle toothache may be much vital to the individual than a debacle that is killing huge number of individuals. Sounds outrageous yet that is the manner by which people are.

Pay attention to activities. Individuals are superheroes in their own accounts caught with falsehoods and horse crap. Try not to care a whole lot to what they say or how they figure everything ought to be. Pay attention to their activities.

• • •

Rationale prompts consistency. Feelings are a completely untrustworthy instrument for direction.

Disregard inherent ability. Uncommonness is generally and procured all of the time. You should feel it when you accomplish something.

Dismissals are ordinary. Do nothing in life just to show somebody or have vengeance. Regardless, do it to build your self-esteem.

Individuals are strange complex creatures. It's not your only task to figure out why individuals acted the manner in which they did.

You are a country. Under any conditions, don't let the attack of your own sovereign country.

Never look for adoration or friendship for culmination. Fulfillment should come all of the time from the inside.

• • •

Screw joy. Joy is a crappy objective. Focus on smugness. Individuals who contend that they would rather not be rich or renowned and just to be content are finished poop chutes. Check out individuals who spin as long as they can remember around unwinding, satisfaction, and amusement. Appreciating however much you can is a useless objective at the expense of the world that won't ever recall you existed.

Screw satisfying individuals. Do nothing in your life only for looking for somebody's approval or social endorsement.

Confidence and sense of pride come from yourself.

Appreciate your legends. Regard their courageous demonstrations. Execute their great perspectives as they considered squarely in your life. However, never under any circumstance aimlessly follow anybody. Indeed, simply appreciate them, won't ever follow. Each visually impaired adherent sees himself as a special case while he is the exemplification of the standard.

• • •

Finally, figure out how to think. In the event that you at any point experience an issue, issue, interest, thought, or anything you need to know about, think all alone. Each snippet of data accessible in any structure came from somebody's psyche. On the off chance that you don't have the foggiest idea, you also have a brain.

Use it to your fullest. You will know the solutions to a considerable lot of the inquiries or if nothing else concoct a thought. Later contrast your reasoning and others by means of books, web, webcast, or any sources accessible. In any case, first and foremost you are all alone. Continuously recollect you, yourself, and doing your thought process is the best matter most than anything more. All the other things is auxiliary.

There are likewise a portion of the things that I didn't like about the book. You don't need to constantly utilize swear words to have a strong effect. Once in a while that sounds exceptionally fake. Individuals could want for minimal more profundity in a portion of the issues in which curtness wasn't wanted. There may be numerous different issues and guarantees where Shwetabh has neglected to convey however surely not on this one.

• • •

• • •

Think and Grow Rich

While the title proposes the book is about cash, it's more about a lifestyle. The creator, Napoleon Hill, presents core values for outcome in all everyday issues. Think and Grow Rich looks at the mental influence of positive idea. Napoleon Hill digs into the significance of our idea designs for our prosperity. Napoleon portrays that best individuals from the past consolidated these positive idea strategies with perseverance, training, and strong associates. We will all bomb while looking to get our life objectives, however those able to continue to attempt will become effective.

> "*"Set your mind on a definite goal and observe how quickly the world stands aside to let you pass." – Napoleon Hill*"

The method for becoming effective is to know what you need to accomplish. Without clear objectives, we can't begin our excursion towards progress. Consequently, Napoleon Hill suggests that individuals start their excursion towards progress by characterizing their own objectives in as exact terms as could really be expected. Assuming you desire to become rich, you ought to characterize how much cash you need to procure by a specific age. Financial and time-explicit objectives will permit you to have a reasonable comprehension of the amount you should contribute to achieving this objective.

• • •

Subsequent to recognizing an objective and giving it a time period, you will then, at that point, need to layout an arrangement. This arrangement should consolidate a bit by bit way to deal with achieving your last objective. When you have this arrangement, you really want to act. Begin straight away and don't squander a moment.

These proposals will assist with keeping you spurred and zeroed in on the following objective you want to zero in on to acquire your general objective.

Napoleon clarifies you can achieve what you look however long you clutch your cravings. In any case, this doesn't mean you should want the result. For instance, just wanting for cash will waste your time. All things considered, you should become fanatical about creating successful plans and achievable objectives that will assist you with your ideal result. One of my cherished statement from the book is

"There is a difference between WISHING for a thing and being READY to receive it. No one is ready for a thing, until he believes he can acquire it. The state of mind must be BELIEF, not mere hope or wish. Open-mindedness is essential for belief."- Napoleon Hill

Relentless confidence is an incredible resource for have. As indicated by Napoleon, people who have an immovable confidence are for the most part the individuals who will take the necessary steps to accomplish their objectives. This is on the grounds that you can't make progress without self-assurance.

• • •

Napoleon gives the case of Mahatma Gandhi to help the force of confidence and fearlessness. Gandhi didn't approach the

common instruments of influence: cash and the military. All things being equal, he had an immovable conviction that he could lead his nation, India, to independence from British provincial rule. This conviction permitted him to foster a huge impact over his kinsmen and accordingly flash a change.

We are the same as Gandhi. Assuming that we can saddle an unfaltering faith in ourselves and our capacity to accomplish our objectives, we can accomplish anything.

• • •

• • •

Paulo Coelho's The Alchemist

The Alchemist is a story that will motivate you to pay attention to your heart and follow your fantasies, something we as a whole need to do! To top that up, the one of a kind vision and otherworldliness of Paulo Coelho will be a helpful encounter. It is no big surprise why this book is viewed as perhaps the best book for novices. The story is about a Shepherd kid from Spain whose name is Santiago. He continues to get the very dream about treasures that are lying in the Pyramids of Egypt. He sets out on an excursion to follow his fantasy in the wake of meeting an old lord who offers him enchantment stones and counsel. Santiago crosses the Mediterranean and

• • •

Sahara to track down his fortunes in Egypt and furthermore achieve his own legend which is his motivation throughout everyday life. The book subtleties his excursion and the different experiences that he encounters while following his fantasy. All through the excursion, Santiago meets many new individuals and a ton of trouble which at last assists him with learning and develop the whole way. Does he track down the fortunes in the Pyramids of Egypt.

• • •

The book shows that the excursion to your predetermination is just about as significant as the actual fate. I love the amazing way the book stresses on the significance of confidence, trust and otherworldliness through the account of a normal kid. I think this book requests to everybody since we as a whole have dreams and here and there we simply need somebody to let us know that they might materialize.

> “*“You came so that you could learn about your dreams,” said the old woman. “And dreams are the language of God. When he speaks in our language, I can interpret what he has said. But if he speaks in the language of the soul, it is only you who can understand – The Alchemist*”

The Alchemist has numerous illustrations and pieces of motivation sprinkled all through the story

> "***"And, when you want something, the entire universe conspires in helping you to achieve it."*** *— Paulo Coelho, the Alchemist*"

When we want something in life, then it's our responsibility to get up and do something about it. Too often in life, we let fate decide our day to day actions and hope all too much that things will work out in the end. Here's a small excerpt from the book which captures the quintessence of this little thought. This statement was likewise used in a Bollywood film named Om shanti om , "Kehte hain agar kisi cheez ko dil se chaho ... to poori kainath use tumse milane ki koshish mein lag jaati hai".

> "***"There is only one thing that makes a dream impossible to achieve: the fear of failure."*** *— Paulo Coelho, The Alchemist*"

A reminder to continue to push forward regardless difficulties we face. Since toward the day's end, we just miss the shots we don't take. So continue dreaming and continue to attempt until your objectives become a reality.

CHAPTER VIII

Little Things

Let me start this chapter with this short story, explaining a moral beautifully.

There was a college student who was always silent and alone. He generally appeared piece apprehensive and didn't have any companions. His educator saw this and one day requested that he meet after class.

When student went to see teacher, teacher said to him, "I see that you are frequently exceptionally tranquil. Neither do you converse with anybody nor you show interest in anything and its effect can be seen in your studies too. What is the reason for this?

Student replied, "Sir, I had truly challenging life. I needed to confront a few extremely tragic occurrences in my day to day existence and I continue to contemplate them. In light of this I'm not ready to focus on anything and don't want to converse with anybody."

Teacher carefully listened to student story then thought for a while and invited student to his home. On decided day, student reached teacher's home on time. "Would you like some lemonade?" teacher asked him. Student hesitatingly replied, "Yes." Teacher went inside and while preparing lemonade, he deliberately added more salt and kept quantity of sugar low. Teacher bought lemonade for him. Student made a strange face, as soon as he drank a sip of that lemonade.

Seeing this teacher asked, "What happened? You didn't like it?" Student replied, "It's just there is a bit too much salt in it..." Teacher stopped him and said, "Oh... You can't drink it... I will throw it away." After saying this, as teacher was lifting the glass to take away, student stopped him and said, "Sir, you don't need to throw it away. It have just bit of extra salt in it, if we add a little more sugar then it will be perfectly fine to drink."

Listening to this teacher smiled and said, “I needed this to hear from you. Presently, contrast what is going on and your life.

Now understand this, to improve the taste of lemonade, we do not remove salt from it but we can fix its taste only by adding more sugar to it.

Likewise, we can’t separate sad occasions from our life that have as of now happened to us however we can delete old harshness and distress by adding pleasantness of good involvement with our life. On the off chance that you continue to cry about your past, neither your current will be correct nor will the future be brilliant." When teacher was finished talking, student realized his mistake and vowed to give the right direction to his life.

So the moral is that Often, We keep looking at the closed door for so long that, we do not even pay attention to good things happening around us. One should learn to forget about past sad experiences and try to give new direction to life.

• • •

Our god opens seven doors, if he closes one. But we’re so struck in that one door, that we don’t be bother to look up to those seven. We are so caged in our daily up and downs, downs and downs i would say, that it has become a habit for all of us to live with it. We ourselves don’t want a change, we don’t want a path less travelled, and we don’t want a difficult path leading to good endings, instead an easy one which leads to bad and depressed situations.

Life is an exciting ride of ups and many downs, and everybody faces it. It is possible that somebody adequately rich to give it with effectively or somebody who exacerbates it by self-destructive circumstances.

The issue is we aggravate it by getting into the snare, by saying "my life is a hellfire', "I need to kick the bucket", "I can’t manage it", we attempt to acknowledge that this is intended for us, this is an everlasting reality of my life. I can’t change this neither can anybody. Indeed, No one can help you except for you, FACE IT, rather than running. We will talk about this in the forthcoming part. We need to make ourselves so solid that we can change any hindrance into an open door.

• • •

Back in school you must have heard this story of a farmer and his donkey One day a farmer's donkey fell down into a well. The animal cried piteously for hours as the farmer tried to figure out what to do. Finally, he concluded the animal was old and the very much required to have been concealed at any rate it simply wasn't worth the effort to recover the jackass. He welcomed every one of his neighbors to come over and help him. They generally got a digging tool and start to scoop soil into the well. Right away, the jackass acknowledged what was occurring and cried frightfully. Then, at that point, incredibly, he calmed down.

A couple of digging tool stacks later, the rancher at long last peered down the well and was surprised at what he saw. With each digging tool of soil that fell on his back, the jackass was accomplishing something astonishing. He

would shake it off and make a stride up. As the rancher's neighbors kept on scooping soil on top of the animal, he would shake it off and make a stride up.

Pretty soon, everybody was flabbergasted as the jackass moved forward over the edge of the well and jogged off!

Moral - Life will scoop soil on you, a wide range of soil. Try to not to get stalled by it. We can escape the most unfathomable wells by not halting. What's more, by never surrendering! Shake it off and make a stride up!

There are numerous ordinary models, numerous well known individuals you realize who fizzled toward the start however presently they stand on their words. They have accomplished what they guaranteed once in their lives. They utilized the chance of disappointment and turned their dread, their pitiful feelings into an excursion of joy.

• • •

An affluent man lived in a city. He was an extremely enormous finance manager and he was not shy of everything except still he was concerned and anxious all the time. On one occasion he went to his Hermitage to meet the sage in a town. The man told his concern to the wise that he has no deficiency of everything except still he is stressed all the time.

The sage heard his concern and said - come tomorrow, I will let you know how to remain cheerful and effortless.

The man arrived at the Hermitage of the sage simultaneously the following day. He saw that the sage was searching for something outside his Hermitage.

The individual said – savant (sage) what are you searching for? May I help you! The sage said - I am searching for my ring, which is lost.

Hearing this, that individual likewise begun looking for his ring with the sage. Indeed, even in the wake of looking from here onward, indefinitely quite a while, the ring was not found, then, at that point, the individual asked the sage - where did your ring fall?

The sage said - My ring fell in the cabin of the Hermitage, however it is extremely dull there, so I am searching for the ring outside the Hermitage.

The individual asked with shock - while your ring fell in the cabin, for what reason would you say you are watching over here???

The sage said - this is the answer for your concern...

Satisfaction is inside you; however you are searching for it in cash and unfamiliar products. The whole ocean is inside you, yet at the same time you are searching for water outside with a spoon. Cash or property is significant throughout everyday life, except bliss can't be purchased uniquely with cash.

• • •

• • •

• • •

"HAPPINESS IS A CHOICE"

An elderly person lived in the town. He was one of the most awful individuals on the planet. The entire town was burnt out on him, he was generally bleak, continually griped and forever was feeling terrible. The more he lived, the more bile was becoming and the more harmful were

his words. Individuals stayed away from him, since his adversity became infectious. It was even unnaturally and offending to be content close to him. He made the sensation of misery in others.

Be that as it may, at some point, when he got eighty years of age, something unbelievable occurred. Immediately everybody heard the gossip: "An Old Man is

blissful today, he doesn't say anything negative about anything, grins, and, surprisingly, his face is cleaned up". The entire town assembled. An elderly person was inquired:

- What befell you?

- Not much.. - he replied. - Eighty years I've been pursuing bliss, and it was pointless. And afterward... I chose to live without bliss and simply appreciate life... That is the reason I am cheerful at this point!

• • •

• • •

• • •

HAPPY DERVISH

Once, a shah was riding in his cart through the town, glancing through the window at the rushing individuals. Unexpectedly, he saw a forlorn dervish sitting in the group, who was grinning and looking cheerful about something. The dervish was dressed ineffectively, and with the exception of the saucer for hand-outs and a street script he had nothing else other than him. The shah street past him and before long failed to remember what he saw.

Following a couple of days, the shah needed to go the same way once more, where he saw a similar dervish once more, totally cheerful, napping with joyfully shut eyes.

The following day, shah picked the same way deliberately, to check whether the dervish will be in his place and again the picture was something very similar. Charmed, shah was going the same way consistently and each time he tracked down the dervish in a similar soul.

At long last, incapable to stand it any longer, shah emerged from the cart and tended to the imperturbable dervish with these words, "For what reason would you say you are continuously grinning? Pretty much consistently I

see you here and it appears to be that you are totally blissful."

"Precisely, my lord." said the dervish happily.

Shah was amazed and inquired, "For what reason would you say you are blissful? Do you have any cash?"

"I have nothing, my lord. Perhaps during the day a smidgen will fall in for food."

"Do you have a home or a family?"

"Neither this and nor that. I meander the world as the breeze."

"Perhaps then, at that point, you have great heath?"

"By no means, my lord, from the cold of the night my bones expert regularly and practically each of my teeth have dropped out."

"What makes you so blissful then, at that point? Tell me. Perhaps your formula for satisfaction will be valuable to me. I have everything, except I'm troubled."

"God never sends more difficulties for one individual that he can't deal with. Furthermore, troubles an individual just with those conditions, which at that point, are generally valuable for his turn of events. The conditions wherein the individual is - is the spot for spiritualization. I acknowledge that the best thing for me currently is the thing I am, the place where I am and what's going on with me. I acknowledge it with appreciation and a grin, if important with obstruction and tolerance, and if conceivable, I attempt to comprehend what God is attempting to tell me with it and in which heading would it be advisable for me I move with my turn of events. Its acknowledgment doesn't make me totally cheerful, however I have a reasonable skyline opening

before me, liberated from the blustery shades and loaded up with the radiant light of mindfulness."

• • •

• • •

• • •

Here are some life advices from experienced individuals.

Begin Saving for future

A many individuals battle to set aside cash, take care of obligation, or even skirt a shopping binge. However, spending shrewdly works on individuals' satisfaction. Individuals feel content when they are monetarily steady, yet research additionally shows that when individuals burn through cash on stuff, their bliss diminishes.

• • •

Cut poisonous individuals from your life

It seems like good judgment, yet many battle with cutting off awful friendships. Analyst says that individuals can be

in such a daze and their life is so occupied, they simply continue to get things done with individuals who are not great with themsaid , on the off chance that they won't treat you benevolent and humanely, you need to continue on. These depleting, unpleasant connections tremendously affect the nature of individuals' lives.

• • •

Focus in on your wellbeing

While youthful grown-ups could feel powerful, skipping exercises, noshing on unhealthy food, and celebrating until the hours shortly before dawn begin to cause significant damage in your 30s. There is an association between a sound body and a solid enthusiastic state.

• • •

Be humane to yourself

Manson said that Your 30s is the point at which the genuine disillusionment in your life appears, I believe that is a battle that a many individuals manage and they fault themselves. Perhaps you didn't get that huge advancement. Or on the other hand your marriage self-destructed. Or on the other hand you're not the

individual you figured you would be. Be that as it may, figuring out how to excuse and be benevolent to themselves assisted individuals with tolerating the mistake and appreciate life.

• • •

Never lament facing a challenge

Whenever individuals talk about something they lament in the previous week, many notice something they attempted, however fizzled at achieving.

Whenever somebody asks individuals in their 60s what they lament from their lives, they frequently say not taking a stab at something they generally needed to attempt, like another food, learning a language, voyaging more, or exchanging careers. Maddux all-around said that, "they lament not having faced the challenge,".

• • •

Live at the time

Here and there individuals stay previously, ruminating about the what the future held. Some of the time they plan a lot for the future, continuously expecting a genuinely new thing. While it's great to think about botches and consider the future, it becomes tricky when individuals stall out previously or future. They pass up encountering life.

• • •

• • •

• • •

Allow me to recount to you a story and get you cheer.

There was a man who had four children. He needed his children to figure out how to not pass judgment on things excessively fast. So he sent them each on a mission, thus, to proceed to take a gander at a pear tree that was a huge span away. The primary child went in the colder time of year, the second in the spring, the third in summer, and the most youthful child in the fall. At the point when they had all proceeded to return, he assembled them to depict what they had seen. The principal child said that the tree was appalling, bowed, and wound. The subsequent child said no - it was covered with green buds and brimming with guarantee.

The third child dissented, he said it was weighed down with blooms that smelled so sweet and looked so excellent, it was the most effortless thing he had at any point seen. The last child contradicted every one of them; he said it was ready and hanging with organic product, brimming with life and satisfaction. The man then, at that point, disclosed to his children that they were OK, since they had each seen yet one season in the tree's life. He let them know that you can't pass judgment on a tree, or an individual, by just one season, and that the substance of what their identity is - and the delight, bliss, and love that come from that life - must be estimated toward the end, when every one of the seasons are up.

Assuming you surrender when it's colder time of year, you will miss the guarantee of your spring, the excellence of your late spring, satisfaction of your fall. Try not to pass judgment on a day to day existence by one troublesome season. Try not to let the torment of one season obliterate the delight of the remainder. These days we get discouraged with such ease, simply a terrible second or an influx of bitterness and we are down to judging and destroying our entire day on it. Our age is one of the most vulnerable from hearts, we treat somethings so in a serious way that we wind up getting discouraged. That is the reason a ton of number of our ages are discouraged and miserable. Make an effort not to treat things so in a serious way that it can influence your wellbeing. Simply hang tight for the time, things will improve. Simply stand by and reflect.

• • •

• • •

• • •

Value Yourselves

A notable speaker got going his course by holding up a $20 note. In the room of 200, he inquired, "Who might like this $20 greenback?"

Hands began going up.

He said, "I will give this $20 to one of you above all, let me do this." He continued to fold the dollar note up.

He then, at that point, inquired, "Who actually needs it?"

Still the hands were up high.

"Well," he answered, "Consider the possibility that I do this?" And he dropped it on the ground and began to crush it into the floor with his shoe.

He got it, presently totally folded and grimy. "Presently who actually needs it?" Still the hands went out of sight.

"My companions, you have all taken in an entirely important illustration. Regardless I did to the cash, you actually needed this is on the grounds that it didn't diminish in esteem. It was as yet worth $20.

Commonly in our lives, we are dropped, folded, and ground into the soil by the choices we make and the conditions that come our direction.

We feel like we are useless. Yet, regardless has occurred for sure will occur, you won't ever lose your worth. You are exceptional -

Don't at any point fail to remember it!

Satisfaction, an inclination basically everybody is looking for, however many battle to genuinely find. Perhaps this is a direct result of the manner in which they go about it; the vast majority will more often than not naturally suspect "When I arrive at this objective I'll be cheerful," or "When I get this advancement I'll at last be blissful," or "When I at long last find 'The one' I will be so cheerful' and they invest such a lot of energy and exertion arranging and pursuing these objectives that they fail to remember that joy doesn't come as an objective, it's really found in the seemingly insignificant details all through the excursion. In the event that you can't partake in the excursion, then, at that point, ultimately when you come to that objective you endeavored to get to, you'll feel impermanent happiness until you consider another objective that you really want to reach to be content once more. A senseless game's played where in the end satisfaction is a hallucination it looks genuine, however when you get to it, its short lived and vanishes.

Rather than continuously going after the impossible dream, begin zeroing in on the little subtleties of your life. Those are your passes to a more joyful life, and you'll arrive when you figure out how to FOCUS in on tracking down bliss in the easily overlooked details.

• • •

• • •

• • •

The Importance of Finding Joy in the Little Things

Rather than continuously going after the impossible dream, begin zeroing in on the little subtleties of your life. Those are your passes to a more joyful life, and you'll arrive when you figure out how to zero in on tracking down satisfaction in the easily overlooked details.

Not certain how to begin on tracking down delight in the easily overlooked details? Straightforward! Begin by taking a gander at kids, since they're probably the best illustration of individuals who track down satisfaction in the least difficult things. At the point when you're around kids you're normally welcomed with energetic giggling, fun stories, and astonished heaves at even the littlest things.

When was the last time you cleaned up, or hopped in a puddle, or investigated to track down bugs on the ground? Odds are you presumably don't recollect. Considerably more so presently in this reality where you are continually besieged with things to contrast yourself with (thanks virtual entertainment!). Being so stressed over what you're not, what you want to be for sure you wish you had can prompt bitterness, and even sorrow.

You could say that the key to genuine satisfaction lies in tracking down euphoria in the seemingly insignificant details. At the point when you can in a real sense pause and enjoy the scenery, you are offering yourself the chance to be helped to remember every one of the seemingly insignificant details that gave you pleasure when you were more youthful and that most probable actually do. The seemingly insignificant details in life are regular sources to battle sensations of pity, dread, and void. Yet again it's returning to those seemingly insignificant details where you will track down delight. So how might you begin zeroing in on the seemingly insignificant details in life to track down satisfaction in them? Well for one, it's memorable's critical that every second matters, particularly this second here and right now.This is your life, and you investing in some opportunity to peruse this is now a magnificent positive development. You're enjoying some time off from your bustling day to zero in on you, to peruse something new that got your attention, an easily overlooked detail with a

possibly huge reward.If this book brought back a grin you lost years prior, it will increase in my joy. Make a vow to yourself that you will see each or the most that you would be able "easily overlooked details" occurring in your environmental elements.

Regardless of whether it's basically as little as last drops from a tap. Happiness isn't something that somebody gives us, nor is it something that we must have authorization for. It is a perspective that is made from the inside. We should end up this section by a means to remain cheerful or to make bliss.

• • •

• • •

• • •

Express your accomplishments

"There is happiness in work. There is no joy besides in the acknowledgment that we have achieved something." - Henry Ford

It's not difficult to become involved with everyday life and never invest in some opportunity to ponder the things we have achieved. Every one of us has done a lot of amazing things in our lives.

So consider the possibility that life is flawed at this careful second. Alright it's taking a tiny bit longer with your wellness objectives. Try not to stress that you haven't arrived at the apex of your profession right now.

Interestingly, you are pushing ahead and you're in a preferred position today over you were yesterday.

Begin a diary posting achievements, achievements, and leap forwards you've encountered. In the wake of composing this rundown, pause for a little while to consider everything you've done.

• • •

• • •

Make every moment count

As Steve Jobs broadly said, "Your work will fill an enormous piece of your life, and the best way to be genuinely fulfilled is to do what you accept is extraordinary work. What's more, the best way to extraordinary work is to adore what you do. In the event that you haven't tracked down it yet, continue to look. Try not to settle. Likewise with all issues of the heart, you'll know when you track down it."

Individuals who live the dream and get paid for it will quite often carry on with a more joyful and more useful life; have higher confidence, and better wellbeing.

• • •

• • •

Disregard being awesome and acknowledge yourself with no guarantees

"Assuming that you search for flawlessness, you won't ever be content." - Leo Tolstoy

Individuals frequently act sure and secure around others however where it counts, they're uncertain.

Acknowledge we live in a flawed world and quit contrasting yourself with others (it's not worth the effort to play 'Staying aware of the Joneses'). When you figure out how to acknowledge yourself for what your identity is, life becomes less complex and more serene.

• • •

• • •

Let yourself know today will be wonderful

"Achievement is a perspective. Assuming you need achievement, begin considering yourself a triumph." - Dr. Joyce Brothers

Bliss comes from the inside. Bliss begins with reshaping your attitude to be positive and taking out every bad idea.

Be positive and have faith in yourself, regardless of the obstructions that could hold you up.

• • •

• • •

Incorporate the seemingly insignificant details you love into your everyday life

"Partake in the seemingly insignificant details, for one day you might think back and acknowledge they were the enormous things." - Robert Brault

I'm certain you've heard the platitude, "the seemingly insignificant details in life matter." The seemingly insignificant details are the little and frequently undervalued parts of life that really satisfy us. Rather, it's your morning stroll along the nearby park, going to your dance class, or wearing that outfit that causes you to feel amazing. Plan your life around the little subtleties that give you joy.

• • •

• • •

Escape your usual range of familiarity and become striking

"Move out of your usual range of familiarity. You can develop assuming that you will feel abnormal and awkward when you have a go at a novel, new thing." - Brian Tracy

We can't become what we need to be by residual what we are." - Max Depree

Nothing worth having accompanies a 100 percent assurance of accomplishment, nor would it be a good idea for it. Being willing to face challenges is what's really going on with life.

Living in your usual range of familiarity recoils your reality and gives you limited focus. Rather than thinking, "If by some stroke of good luck I had...," go out on a limb and

perhaps, quite possibly, you'll find the existence you needed 100% of the time.

• • •

• • •

Everybody has 'stuff' happening throughout everyday life

The stuff isn't the issue, the contemplating the stuff is the issue. Your thought process makes how you feel and, thus, which moves you make. Thinking contrarily never helped anybody, so provoking your contemplations to alleviate the burden is basic. Becoming mindful of your considerations truly matters here. Recollect that you are by all account not the only one with anything it is life is tossing at you. Everybody is battling their conflicts, some flop some success, all we really want to accept is that we will succeed toward the end. Each one is managing their concerns, not simply you. You need to acknowledge that life will toss impediments (hardships) to you, yet you need to gather them and construct a realm from it.

• • •

• • •

Nobody leaves alive

Truly, life is intended to be an audacious exciting ride. Next time you have a negative idea, stop and inquire as to whether what you're stressed over will matter in impending years' say a time of 5 years. In the event that the response is indeed, talk about it with somebody who can help you a specialist or an educator yet assuming the response is no, allow yourself five minutes to worry over it and afterward continue on. All that which comes in our day to day existence doesn't mean has an importance or reason. You need to pick regardless of whether it's really great for you.

• • •

• • •

Stress is a self-caused bad dream

But then worrying is the least impact critical thinking procedure in your entire presence. Probably the most ideal way to manage unpleasant circumstances is to be an observer rather than a casualty. Notice things from being an onlooker. Doing this can assist you with placing things into viewpoint remove the feeling from it and, with somewhat point of view, you observe that nothing is ever just about as terrible as you suspect it is. At times the second exacerbates it.

• • •

• • •

Push through the limits

At last, recollect that nobody who changed the world surrendered or adjusted to society's assumptions. Everybody you appreciate continued to push through the limits, battling through the obstructions, developed through the interaction and probable left a mark on the world. They were not unique, very much like us.

The point here is that when we approach life less in a serious way and take a gander at current realities, we can then stop, rethink and continue onward with somewhat less pressure and dread and somewhat more ready and waiting. Recollect that regardless of the amount you could want for something to occur or not, anguishing about it will not do you a touch of good. Regardless of whether things work out as you trusted, don't pressure. Your objective is composed, you don't need to be concerned, all you really want to do is the difficult work.

Life has a strange approach to working out and generally when we give up to the cycle, it takes us farther than any measure of stressing at any point would.

> "" *I never loose. I either win or learn"*
> *-Nelson Mandela* "

• • •

Happiness for some is work, family, kids who will grow up and leave you, a spouse or husband who will turn out to be more similar to a companion than a genuine sweetheart. And afterward one day your work will end as well. what will you do then, at that point?

Truly we have no response for that. Rather we begin giving bogus reasons to ourselves, when the youngsters have grown up, when my better half or my better half has become more my companion than my enthusiastic darling, when I resign then I'll have the opportunity to do what I generally needed to do; voyaging, or whatever other leisure activity that you couldn't do prior.

Do you have any idea that you will have that joy eventually? what in the event that you don't? imagine a scenario in which you're not alive to observe this multitude of things. It's currently or never. Nobody realizes what will occur, we plan things albeit the god is best, all things considered, agonizing over things that you don't know anything about, isn't it odd? or on the other hand foolish I would agree.

• • •

It is great to anticipate future, yet losing the easily overlooked details, the delight, the satisfaction in its anything but really smart. Thus, at last you came as far as possible, I'll be truly appreciative on the off chance that this book can assist you with tracking down your joy. Life is a delightful excursion loaded with affection and torment, you can decide to be an individual who gets discouraged by the troubles of life or rather an individual who can draw out the delight of the other individual.

Bliss makes satisfaction. I might want to end the book with this expression, " Happiness is inside you, you don't need to look anyplace, simply notice and transmit". Remain cheerful. Stay happy. Good Bye.

Author's Note

This "99" is just only a title, it's in our grasp, in our control, to make it up to 999 and counting or we can diminish it to nothing. We make satisfaction, we make our own, and we see these as "little things. it's been an incredible excursion composing these 99 pages of my bliss and offering it to you. Much thanks to you for opening this book, being away from online entertainment regardless of whether it is for some time. I trust this book assists you with observing your joy which has been lost in this contemporary world. Much obliged to YOU. Remain HAPPY.

- Mohd Asad Naqvi

Printed by Libri Plureos GmbH in Hamburg,
Germany